Nature as E

THOUGHT IN THE ACT

~~~~~~

A series edited by
Erin Manning and Brian Massumi

Nature as Event

The Lure of the Possible

DIDIER DEBAISE

Translated by Michael Halewood

DUKE UNIVERSITY PRESS | DURHAM AND LONDON | 2017

Designed by Matthew Tauch
Typeset in Garamond Premier Pro by Copperline Books

Library of Congress Cataloging-in-Publication Data
Names: Debaise, Didier, author.
Title: Nature as event : the lure of the possible /
Didier Debaise ; translated by Michael Halewood.
Other titles: Appât des possibles. English | Thought in the act.
Description: Durham : Duke University Press, 2017. |
Series: Thought in the act
Identifiers: LCCN 2017009715 (print)
LCCN 2017012718 (ebook)
ISBN 9780822369332 (hardcover : alk. paper)
ISBN 9780822369486 (pbk. : alk. paper)
ISBN 9780822372424 (ebook)
Subjects: LCSH: Whitehead, Alfred North, 1861–1947. |
Philosophy of nature.
Classification: LCC B1674.W354 (ebook) |
LCC B1674.W354 D4313 2017 (print) | DDC 113—dc23
LC record available at https://lccn.loc.gov/2017009715

FU / US

Translated with the financial support of the University
Foundation of Belgium.

Cover art: Ernst Haeckel, *Kunstformen der Natur*,
plate 85: Ascidiae. Leipzig und Wien: Verlag des
Bibliographischen Instituts, 1899–1904.

Contents

Introduction

~~~~~

Our experience of nature is threatened by a growing tension between, on the one hand, the modern conception of nature that we have inherited, permeating each of our thoughts, and, on the other, current ecological changes.[1] It seems that this tension has today reached a point of no return. The concepts we deploy, the abstractions we construct, our very modes of thought are no longer able to deepen or develop our experience of nature; they only obscure its meaning.

This book aims to outline the conditions for a different way of thinking about nature by rekindling certain propositions that can be found in the philosophy of Whitehead. This return to Whitehead might appear surprising. Although his work on cosmology has been hailed by philosophers as diverse as Bergson, Dewey, Merleau-Ponty, and Deleuze, beyond these specific instances his work has remained little known and has had little influence.[2] It is perhaps this position on the margins of the principal movements in contemporary philosophy that explains the renewed interest in Whitehead's thought over recent years. It seems that the reasons for his marginal status are precisely those that now make his work so relevant, as if the strangeness of the questions that animated him, and the speculative and cosmological claims that pervade his work, were inaudible for a time but have today, and against all expectations, become central to current concerns.[3] By developing recent texts on Whitehead's philosophy, I will suggest that his work provides new tools for thinking the modern invention of nature and also establishes the conditions for going beyond this, moving toward what I would like to call a "universal mannerism."[4]

This book, therefore, has two aims: to show that the modern conception of nature does not express any genuine ontological position (dualist or monist) but is essentially *operative*, and it is the status of these operations that needs to be traced and questioned if we want to understand how a specific representation of nature has come to impose itself upon us. The heart of this operation, its constitutive gesture, its hallmark, is the division of nature into two heterogeneous modes of existence, whose paradigmatic expression is the difference between "primary" and "secondary" qualities. It is from this distinction that all of the divisions between beings, all the oppositions between their attributes and their aspects, are derived: existence and value; real nature and apparent nature; fact and interpretation. The second aim involves introducing the term "universal mannerism" to indicate a way of overcoming the strictures imposed by this operation. I want to argue that being and manner are intermingled and that there are as many modes of existence in nature as there are ways of experiencing, of feeling, of making sense, and of granting importance to things. The sense of value, of importance, and of purpose—which in our modern experience of nature come under the notion of "psychic additions," of projections by humans of something onto nature that it would otherwise lack—are to be found everywhere, from the most elementary forms of life of microorganisms to reflexive consciousness. The speculative question that runs through this book is as follows: how to grant due importance to the multiplicity of ways of being within nature?

CHAPTER ONE

The Cosmology of the Moderns

~~~~~~

My primary aim is to take up, while also trying to update, Whitehead's protest against what he calls "the bifurcation of nature." Although this phrase might, at first sight, appear a little puzzling, it designates the collection of experiential, epistemological, and political operations that were present at the origin of the modern conception of nature, a concept whose effects can still be felt today. Before moving on to a full analysis, I will start by providing some context.

The phrase "bifurcation of nature" appears in Whitehead's first truly philosophical book, *The Concept of Nature*, published in 1920. By this time, Whitehead had already produced an important body of work. He was well known for his work in mathematics, especially for co-writing *Principia Mathematica* with Bertrand Russell. However, *The Concept of Nature* marked a turning point. This is the first text in which Whitehead sets out the task that will characterize all his later philosophical developments: "The object of the present volume and of its predecessor is to lay the basis of a natural philosophy which is the necessary presupposition of a reorganised speculative physics."[1] It is certainly possible to find ideas in Whitehead's earlier texts that lead up to *The Concept of Nature*, notably in *An Inquiry concerning the Principles of Natural Knowledge*, which appeared in 1919. But it is only in this text from 1920 that Whitehead starts a systematic inquiry into the abstractions of science, one that will later develop and extend to cover all aspects of experience, most notably in his magnum opus, *Process and Reality*. For the moment, the important point to note is that in this text from 1920 Whitehead presents himself as a scientist, declaring a fundamental crisis in his discipline, namely the natural sciences. Getting beyond this crisis will involve a complete reorientation. This is one of the constant obsessions of his work, and Whitehead clarifies his point in a later text, *Science and the Modern World*: "The progress of science has now reached a turning point. The stable foundations of physics have broken up: also for the first time physiology is asserting itself as an effective body of knowledge, as distinct from a scrap-heap. The old foundations of scientific thought are becoming unintelligible. Time, space, matter, material, ether, electricity, mechanism, organism, configuration, structure, pattern, function, all require reinterpretation."[2]

This situating of bifurcation within the context of modern science does not, however, restrict its importance to one particular field. The whole of modern philosophy is touched by the error of bifurcation. Whitehead says no more about this, and it is up to us to grasp the implications for ourselves, including the shift from modern science to the whole of modern natural philosophy. Nevertheless, two elements can be identified in this brief passage that will help clarify the status of bifurcation. First, importance appears to be relativized. It is not a constant that runs through the history of the experience of nature, setting itself up as some transcendental form, of which different conceptions of nature are merely figures or expressions. Instead, importance is historically situated. It would certainly be wrong to state that there is one moment that represents the absolute genesis of bifurcation, for the historical influences are numerous, and its conceptual conditions are rooted in the distant past. However, in no way does this vitiate the idea that this bifurcation is, in its efficacy, genuinely historically located. Implicitly, it is a matter of an epochal, or historical, theory of nature. Second, Whitehead grants bifurcation a field of application that seems, a priori, to be unlimited, as he states that the modern period is "entirely coloured" by it.[3]

The concept of bifurcation originated in the development of modern science. There is no doubt about this. It was during an analysis of the invention of the modern science, and its particular place in the history of science, that Whitehead coined the term, to identify its constitutive operation. Nevertheless, even if its origin can be located in experimental practices, the question of bifurcation is not restricted to one specific domain of modern experience: it is the origin of a global transformation at all levels of experience. In other texts, Whitehead talks of a "predominant interest"[4] that operates as both the source and the expression of any cosmology, affecting all dimensions, from the epistemological to aesthetic and moral experiences of nature. It is at this point that he attributes a first function to philosophy, one that will subsequently configure its other functions: "Philosophy, in one of its functions, is the critic of cosmologies. It is its function to harmonise, refashion, and justify divergent intuitions as to the nature of things. It has to insist on the scrutiny of the ultimate ideas, and on the retention of the whole of the evidence in shaping our cosmological scheme."[5]

Thus, these two aspects coincide: locating bifurcation within a particular epoch might seem to reduce its importance by making it "historical," but it enables Whitehead to grant it an unrivalled scope, one which operates at all levels of experience.

The Gesture of Bifurcation

Having clarified the context in which the concept of bifurcation originated, it is now possible to give more detail regarding its constitution and to ask directly: What exactly is the bifurcation of nature? In the very first pages of *The Concept of Nature*, Whitehead provides a definition, in the form of a protest: "What I am essentially protesting against is the bifurcation of nature into two systems of reality, which, in so far as they are real, are real in different senses. One reality would be the entities such as electrons that are the study of speculative physics. This would be the reality that is there for knowledge; although on this theory it is never known. For what is known is the other sort of reality, which is the byplay of the mind."[6]

This passage has been the subject of a series of misreadings and misunderstandings with regard to how bifurcation should be understood. It is necessary to take this passage at face value, in order to develop a better grasp of what is at stake in the challenge that it makes and to inherit from it in an adequate way. The first impression is that, in one way or another, bifurcation returns us to "dualism." The terminology and the oppositions used certainly seem similar. Does the difference between a "reality which is there for knowledge" and a reality established by "the byplay of the mind" or, equally, between "causal nature" and "apparent nature," not return us to the distinction between extension and thought, between matter and spirit? If this were the case, would bifurcation not simply be a new way of thinking about dualism and, furthermore, a new approach to developing a critique of dualist philosophy, principally that of Descartes, and its influence on the modern epoch? If Whitehead's philosophy is read in this way, it might certainly gain something from its proximity to other critiques of dualism, but it would lose its originality. Yet, it is this reading of bifurcation, as offering a new critique of dualism, that has predominated. It can be found in the lectures that Merleau-Ponty gave on Whitehead's philosophy,[7] and in the work of Jean Wahl,[8] but it is Félix Cesselin who makes the point most starkly: "I think that it is only possible to fully grasp Whitehead's thought by starting with a reading of what he understands by the rejection of the "bifurcation" of nature. The bifurcation of nature is dualism. In particular, it is Cartesian dualism."[9] This interpretation is far from being an isolated case. It expresses most clearly and succinctly what the majority of readers of Whitehead believe they have found in bifurcation.

I would like to suggest a different way of inheriting this concept by affirming *a radical difference between bifurcation and dualism.* This is not to claim that previous readings of bifurcation are wrong, but they have reduced its importance. If the concept of bifurcation is to be given its true force, another approach needs to be taken. In order to substantiate this hypothesis, three elements will be introduced. First, although Whitehead often refers to dualism in his writings, notably Cartesian dualism, he also talks of bifurcation, its constituent elements and its influence in the experience of modernity, without invoking any relationship to dualism. If bifurcation really were just another name for dualism, and Whitehead was trying to outline the constitutive role of the latter in the development of modern science, then why did he not take the time to link them in some way? The most plausible interpretation is that the two problems seemed so different to Whitehead that he did not think it necessary to comment on the distinction. It seems that, for Whitehead, the obvious difference between the two required no explanation. Second, according to Whitehead, the only possible relation is one of an inversion. One of the rare occasions on which Whitehead does link bifurcation and dualism can be found in *Science and the Modern World*, when he writes, "The revival of philosophy in the hands of Descartes and his successors was entirely coloured in its development by the acceptance of the scientific cosmology [the bifurcation of nature] at its face value."[10] This is a particularly important remark that merits a careful reading. Far from identifying bifurcation with dualism, Whitehead is clear that both Cartesian dualism, and dualism more generally, are dependent upon the question of bifurcation. It is Cartesian philosophy that accepts "at its face value" the cosmology of the bifurcation of nature. This rare allusion to the relation between bifurcation and Cartesian philosophy makes Whitehead's position absolutely clear, although he does not draw out its implications. Third, the reading of this passage offered here entails that the notion of bifurcation outlines a concept that is broader and more fundamental than that of dualism, which, ultimately, is only one of its manifestations. Taken in the most direct, literal, sense, these two notions designate fundamentally different realities. The notion of bifurcation manifests the idea of process, of a movement of differentiation. It is the trajectory through which nature is divided into two distinct branches. The phrase says nothing about how this division occurred, and even less about that which produced it, but it already points to a primary and important difference with respect to dualism. If dualism is understood in terms of a duality of substances, regardless of how these are characterized, bifurcation indicates something very different, namely, how a single reality, nature, came to be divided into two distinct realms.

I will use the terms "gesture"[11] and "operation" to account for this division of nature, as they seem to capture most accurately the particular character of bifurcation. The fundamental question is not that of knowing whether nature is genuinely, in itself, composed of two realms, each with distinct attributes. Rather, it is a question of the means by which the differentiation of these attributes was established. It is the modus operandi of the division, the gesture of the constitution of this division, that needs to be addressed, not its consequences, as expressed in a dualist vision of nature.

As such, the origin of bifurcation should be sought not in the relations between thought and extension, mind and body, the real and the apparent, but in the characteristics of bodies themselves. Bifurcation gains its sense at the intersection of a range of questions: What is a natural body? What are its qualities and how do we experience it? Can we identify characteristics that are common to the multiplicity of physical and biological bodies, and what would these be? These are the same questions as those posed by the distinction between the primary and secondary qualities of bodies that lies at the origin of the modern conception of nature, of which we are still the heirs.

One of the classic texts that most clearly states the difference between the qualities of bodies, and provides the basis for Whitehead's development of his critique of bifurcation, is Locke's *An Essay concerning Human Understanding*. Of course, Locke's *Essay* cannot claim to have invented the problem. For example, Boyle's book *The Origin of Forms and Qualities according to the Corpuscular Philosophy*, published in 1666, undoubtedly influenced Locke's thought, and this text contains the essentials of the difference between the qualities of bodies. However, what is important at this stage is not an outline of the history of bifurcation, as such. Rather, the task at hand is to trace its dispersed invention and how it became consolidated within both experimental practice and those texts that provided its conceptual expression. Locke's *Essay*, particularly the chapter "Some Further Considerations concerning Our Simple Ideas" is, in this sense, paradigmatic. Locke constructs the distinction as follows:

> First such as are *Primary qualities* utterly inseparable from the body. [...] These I call original or primary qualities of body, which I think we may observe to produce simple ideas in us, viz. solidity, extension, figure, motion or rest, and number. Secondly, such qualities which in truth are nothing in the objects themselves but power to produce various sensations in us by their primary qualities, i.e. by the bulk, figure, texture, and motion of their insensible parts, as colours, sounds, tastes, etc. These I call secondary qualities.[12]

In this passage, Locke assigns the qualities of bodies to two different realms. First, there are *primary qualities*, which are "inseparable from the body." The term "primary" should be taken in its strong sense, as it indicates that these qualities are fundamental to the body and characterize its deepest reality. Primary qualities express the purified state of the body, unadorned by any variations to which it could be subjected. The qualities that Locke lists in this passage all refer to a physico-mathematical order: solidity, extension, figure [number], motion, and rest. As such, it is now possible to give a first response to the question "What is a natural body?" It is a particular articulation between physicomathematical qualities. Locke gives an example that has become well known: "Take a grain of wheat, divide it into two parts; each part has still *solidity, extension, figure*, and *mobility*: divide it again, and it retains still the same qualities and so divide it on, till the parts become insensible; they must retain still each of them all those qualities."[13] The phenomenal variations, such as the color of the grain, its particular texture, the sensations that we have of it, in no way undermine the status of the primary qualities with which they are associated. Even when division renders a body imperceptible, so that it falls short of producing an empirical experience, because these qualities are of a specific kind and refer to what might be called a nonsubjective aspect of nature, they must still be constitutive of all experiences of bodies. This is why it is necessary to insist that without these primary qualities, nature would be "soundless, scentless, colourless; merely the hurrying of material, endlessly, meaninglessly."[14] It would be wrong to think that this is an outdated conceptual approach; its legacy can still be found in contemporary science. As Whitehead puts it, in *Science and the Modern World*:

> There persists, however, throughout the whole period the fixed scientific cosmology which presupposes the ultimate fact of an irreducible brute matter, or material, spread throughout space in a flux of configurations. In itself such a material is senseless, valueless, purposeless. It just does what it does do, following a fixed routine imposed by external relations which do not spring from the nature of its being. It is this assumption that I call "scientific materialism."

Also it is an assumption which I shall challenge as being entirely unsuited to the scientific situation at which we have now arrived.[15]

The critique of bifurcation is, therefore, linked to a radical critique of materialism. Raymond Ruyer, one of the most original readers of Whitehead, gives what he calls a "quaint," almost "humorous," image of the materialism that Whitehead is criticizing. Recalling Carlyle, he imagines a law court, as viewed through the eyes of a materialist who is an heir to the bifurcation of nature: "It undergoes a curious metamorphosis, a sort of denuding [. . .]. The halo of meaning, essence, values, all that which for an ordinary spectator transfigures the materiality of the scene, and yet is almost overlooked, all this dissipates like a mist."[16] What remains, for the materialist, is the functioning "of a kind of complicated mechanism, fully given in the present and in space, where morsels of matter push one another. A man speaks: the state of his brain controls the physical formulation of his speech: the vibrations of air modify other elements of the nervous system and control movements or the preparations for movement. No intention, no purpose, guides the phases of the scene, since intention is no more than the present state of the brain."[17]

Ruyer caricatures this tendency of materialism, a materialism that can be termed physicalist, in order to draw out other possible routes, other approaches and directions. Similarly, Whitehead's criticism of scientific materialism is linked to his affirmation of a superior materialism, a materialism that he sometimes calls "organicist,"[18] which, far from returning to bifurcation, has connections with the philosophies of thinkers such as Diderot and Spinoza.[19] The materialism that Whitehead critiques is one which posits, on the one hand, "a material [which] is senseless, valueless, purposeless" with, on the other, phenomenal experiences that, since they must be given their due place, receive all the qualities excluded from this purified matter. It will be remembered that both primary qualities, and the materialism that follows from them, want to reject all so-called subjective elements, that is to say, all the sensations, values, and modes of being that somehow mask natural bodies.

Having set out this primary realm of bodies, Locke turns to the second realm, which he indeed calls "secondary." In the passage cited above, he gives some examples: colors, sounds, taste, and so on. It is important to note a subtle point here. Secondary qualities are not described as simple projections by the mind onto bodies, as if the perceiving subject projects forms or impressions that are completely external or unrelated to the bodies that are experienced (the law court in the previous example). This is the difficulty presented at the end of the quotation taken from Locke's *Essay*. Here he writes that secondary qualities are nothing other than the "power to produce various sensations in us by their primary qualities."[20] Locke is invoking a complex relation of dependence and difference. The mind is clearly involved, since it is in the activity of perception that primary qualities are altered, forming the different aspects by which we experience them, but the mind's capacity is intimately linked to the *power* of primary qualities to affect. In short, although secondary qualities are radically distinct from primary qualities, they are derived from them, as they are an aspect of them. Secondary qualities constitute what might be called the domain of "psychic additions." It is through such an addition that materialism is able to give a place to subjective experience: "We perceive the red billiard ball at its proper time, in its proper place, with its proper motion, with its proper hardness, and with its proper inertia. But its redness and its warmth, and the sound of the click as a cannon is made off it are psychic additions, namely, secondary qualities which are only the mind's way of perceiving nature."[21]

In the context of bifurcation, the theory of psychic additions enables a link to be established between primary and secondary qualities. This theory appears to give a place to the phenomenal experience of bodies by inscribing the latter in an order of nonphenomenal qualities. In our immediate experience, we encounter only hybrid qualities, ones derived from the power of bodies but altered by the mind. In this sense, and in more contemporary terms, it is possible to reread the previous examples and state, "What is given in perception is the green grass. This is an object which we know as an ingredient in nature. The theory of psychic additions would treat the greenness as a psychic addition furnished by the perceiving mind, and would leave to nature merely the molecules and the radiant energy which influence the mind towards that perception."[22]

What is fundamental is that the distinction between primary and secondary qualities starts from an empirical base—the perception of a grain of wheat, the red billiard ball, the green grass, the law court—in order to then differentiate between nonperceptual qualities and those subjective qualities which are supposedly derived from the former, while also expressing them. This is the heart of the operation of bifurcation. It is here that the moment of bifurcation is located. Starting with immediate experience, bifurcation operates by splitting such experience into two regimes of existence. In doing so, it takes that which constitutes the primary experience of nature and places it into a derivate, phenomenal realm. Once this bifurcation is established, once the two regimes are stabilized and subjective experience is rendered as epiphenomenal, it is possible to state that even if a fundamental knowledge of primary qualities is permanently postponed *in fact*, such knowledge would, *by right*, allow for knowledge of secondary qualities, by derivation, even if secondary qualities are the only things that we know, practically speaking. As a result, there is no need for an exploration of bodily perceptions, as such. On this basis, it is possible to define the process of knowledge that is at the root of all epistemologies that are derived from the operation of bifurcation as an operation of correlation between secondary qualities (simple appearances), and primary qualities (which are purely conjectural).

Another way of phrasing this theory which I am arguing against is to bifurcate nature into two divisions, namely into the nature apprehended in awareness and the nature which is the cause of awareness. The nature which is the fact apprehended in awareness holds within it the greenness of the trees, the song of the birds, the warmth of the sun, the hardness of the chairs, and the feel of the velvet. The nature which is the cause of awareness is the conjectured system of molecules and electrons which so affects the mind as to produce the awareness of apparent nature. The meeting point of these two natures is the mind, the causal nature being influent and the apparent nature being effluent.[23]

The conclusion to be drawn is that the modern invention of nature did not originate in an ontological position, either dualist or monist, but in *local operations* of the qualification of bodies. The ontology of the moderns comprises the manner in which they have attempted to express the permanently repeated gesture of dividing bodies and their qualities while continually masking this very operation. In short, this ontology presupposes the gestures, techniques, and operations of division.

The same applies to experimental apparatuses. Thus, for example, Galileo's invention of an inclined plane, described in his notes published in 1608, perfectly illustrates how the operative apparatuses that are at the origin of bifurcation have a preeminence over all those theories that later come to justify it. As Stengers writes in *The Invention of Modern Science*:

> This schema represents an experimental apparatus, in the modern sense of the term, an apparatus of which Galileo is the *author*, in the strong sense of the term, because it is a question of an artificial, premeditated setup that produces "facts of art," artifacts in the positive sense. And the singularity of this apparatus, as we will see, is that it *allows its author to withdraw*, to let the motion *testify* in his place.[24]

The apparatus is thus a construction, signed and dated, a wholly invented artifact, whose function is to introduce a difference between ways of explaining motion. The apparatus does not reproduce a direct observation on a different scale, nor does it generalize and augment a local phenomenon. The experimental apparatus breaks with all direct relations of resemblance, conformity, or reproduction. It certainly does not gain its justification by simply making a purported experience visible. The success of the apparatus is to be found elsewhere: in the withdrawal of its creator in favor of the testimony of motion itself. In this sense, "the fictive world proposed by Galileo is not simply the world that Galileo knows how to interrogate, it is a world *that no one could interrogate differently than he*. It is a world whose categories are *practical* because they are those of an experimental apparatus that he invented."[25] According to the terms in which the problem has been set out so far, it is possible to state that through the construction of an artifact, the apparatus aims to make nature bifurcate into two branches—the primary qualities of nature that express themselves in motion, and the secondary qualities that are the explanations given of such motion—while simultaneously effacing the constructed character of this operation.

I am, therefore, suggesting that the bifurcation between primary and secondary qualities is the constitutive operation of the modern experience of nature. This places my argument firmly within current attempts to give due importance to the debate over such qualities. Thus, for example, in *After Finitude*, Quentin Meillassoux laments that the debate over the difference between primary and secondary qualities has fallen into disuse: "The theory of primary and secondary qualities seems to belong to an irremediably obsolete philosophical past."[26] This is a recurrent theme of the book, as confirmed a few lines later: "For the contemporary reader, such a distinction might appear to be a piece of scholastic sophistry, devoid of any fundamental philosophical import."[27] I fully support Meillassoux with regard to the importance of this debate over the constitution of modern experience. The main aim of the arguments developed in previous pages has been to express, as strongly as possible, the importance of this difference between the qualities of bodies. However, I would like to distance my approach from that of Meillassoux on two points: first, I have attempted to show that the impression that the difference between qualities has fallen into disuse, or appears to belong to a bygone past, does not mean that its effects on contemporary thought have diminished—rather, it clearly remains its condition. This division between qualities continues to have effects while the operations that constitute this split remain in the background, functioning implicitly within all areas of experience, prior to the elaboration of any ontological standpoint. If "rehabilitation," as Meillassoux calls it, makes sense, it is certainly not because it aims to revive a project that has remained bracketed within contemporary thought, since it has never been more effective. Such a "rehabilitation" only makes a genealogical sense; it involves bringing these gestures and operations to the surface, in order to better identify the theoretical and ontological assumptions that they imply. Second, Meillassoux maintains that the condition of a renewal of "thought's relation to the absolute"[28] will find its full expression in a new form of materialism. This is the direction that he takes when posing the question of the current legacy of this differentiation. I have attempted to demonstrate that the materialism that results from bifurcation is essentially a formal one (a discussion of this will be taken up in the following pages). It involves constricting all the forms of existence in nature onto one of the two branches of a purely operative division. These operations have had localized effects, but their reification into a more general ontological form can be achieved only at the expense of fundamental aspects of the plurality of forms of existence in nature. The only reason why it is crucial to return, today, to a clear and sustained analysis of the debate over primary and secondary qualities is as follows: in order to get beyond this opposition and the conception of nature that is derived from it. If a new materialism is to emerge, it will not come from within the legacy of bifurcation, but from going beyond it.

The Localization of Matter

Bifurcation leaves a murky zone in its wake, one produced by its own operations. Since all modern experience of nature inhabits this bifurcation and points toward the primary qualities of bodies, which are both constitutive of experience and yet inaccessible to it, a more detailed investigation into these natural bodies in themselves is necessary. The question of quite what these primary qualities are in themselves is put center stage, dramatized, and intensified to the maximum by this murky zone. But bifurcation leaves open the question of knowing how to characterize bodies when they are extricated from their phenomenal dimension. The operation of bifurcation only repeats, permanently, the separation of the qualities of bodies into various registers—that of physics, the biological and social. But this separation continually leads back to a series of questions that receive no adequate response: What *is* a body when it is separated from its secondary qualities? How can we make sense of such a body, since we only have access to secondary qualities? What kind of knowledge would allow us to penetrate into the interior of these nonobservable qualities? According to the interpretation provided above, the inability to provide a characterization of primary qualities is not a weakness of the modern conception of nature; it is where it draws its strength. It is the dramatization of this difficulty that constitutes this modern conception. It was necessary to push this point to the extreme, in order to give due weight to the second operation that is constitutive of modern cosmology. Whitehead gives it a new name: "the simple location of matter." It is this that will provide the abstractions that are required to deal with natural bodies. I will cite the long passage in which Whitehead describes this:

> To say that a bit of matter has simple location means that, in expressing its spatiotemporal relations, it is adequate to state that it is where it is, in a definite finite region of space, and throughout a definite finite duration of time, apart from any essential reference of the relations of that bit of matter to other regions of space and to other durations of time. Again, this concept of simple location is independent of the controversy between the absolutist and the relativist views of space or of time. So long as any theory of space, or of time, can give a meaning, either absolute or relative, to the idea of a definite region of space, and of a definite duration of time, the idea of simple location has a perfectly definite meaning.[29]

Whitehead appears to affirm that, in the modern conception of nature, the possibility of being localizable, of having a simple location, is a characteristic of matter. It is important not to misunderstand his point. The proposition is more radical than that: matter is *only* localization. This represents the crucial element of the passage. With regard to the question "What is matter in modern experience?," I would offer the response "A *localizable* point." It is a minimal definition, but it has a radical effect. For questions about the origin, form, and nature of matter are replaced by a question of a quite different order—where is it situated? In this sense, it is possible to say, with Ruyer, that "that which characterizes science [. . .] is that it is knowledge of that which is in space and in time."[30] Thus, it is as if the body, detached from "psychic additions," is no more than an element that is localizable in space-time. It is possible to understand "scientific materialism" only if we take into account the circularity of its definition of matter and of space-time, which leads to the reduction of matter to a localizable element. "The characteristic common both to space and time is that matter can be said to be here in space and here in time, or here in space-time, in a perfectly definite sense which does not require for its explanation any reference to other regions of space-time."[31]

There is a multiplicity of here-and-nows that precisely delimit zones of matter and the boundaries that separate it from other areas of the universe. According to this perspective, one space-time is sufficient, in itself, and does not need to make any reference to other space-times. Consequently, the response to the question "What is the world made of?" that emerged in the seventeenth century was as follows: "The world is a succession of instantaneous configurations of matter, or of material, if you wish to include more subtle stuff than ordinary matter, the ether, for example."[32] Whitehead sees Newtonian physics as one of the most important examples of this cosmological outlook: "Newtonian physics is based upon the independent individuality of each bit of matter. Each stone is conceived as fully describable apart from any reference to any other portion of matter. It might be alone in the Universe, the sole occupant of uniform space. But it would still be that stone which it is. Also the stone could be adequately described without any reference to past or future. It is to be conceived fully and adequately as wholly constituted within the present moment."[33]

Whitehead's critique of the notion of "simple location" can be developed by delineating three premises that are fundamental to modernity's cosmology and that need to be analyzed further. The first premise is that *matter can occupy only one space-time*. Clearly, the reason for this is that this premise is based on the idea of *simple* location. This simplicity must be taken literally. It describes the mode of localization, a quality that has a profound place in modern thought. Schematically, it is possible to say that matter is placed *here* in space and, even more so, *now* in time; it is a question not only of the spatial and temporal framework but also of nature itself. Nature is envisaged as a multiplicity of localizable material points that form the bodies and locales of all existence. Thus, Whitehead rejects the first premise of localization and states that the simple existence of matter is a myth or, more precisely, an abstraction that has had disastrous consequences. As Wahl puts it, "Time as a succession of instants does not correspond to anything of which I have any direct knowledge. I can only think of it with the help of metaphors, either as a succession of points on a line, or a set of values of an independent variable in certain differential equations. That of which we are aware is a duration of nature with temporal extension. The present contains antecedents and consequents within it, antecedents and consequents which are themselves temporal extensions."[34] While the division of space and time into points and instants is useful in many cases, it is made possible by the work of an abstraction; when it is generalized and posited as a principle of matter itself it creates innumerable difficulties and false problems. The questioning of this first premise will lead Whitehead to develop a relativistic theory of time and space.

The second premise is that *other modes of existence of matter are exclusively phenomenal*. It is in this premise that simple location most clearly displays its relation to the bifurcation of nature. Indeed, the same gesture of differentiation between two orders of reality can be found here, but now situated in a more technical framework: on one side, the localizable points that constitute matter; on the other, all the derivative forms such as duration, persistence of matter, and the variations and intensifications of existence. This is bifurcation redeployed at another level, with its psychic and phenomenal additions, yet always reducible to the material, brute existence of simple location. This construction "is beautifully simple. But it entirely leaves out of account the interconnections between real things. Each substantial reality is thus conceived as complete in itself, without any reference to any other substantial reality."[35]

The third premise is that *matter is that which is more concrete*. This is the paradox of scientific materialism. Material points, the ultimate existents of matter, which are called upon to occupy a central and primary place in any explanation of nature in general, are unthinkable without a formalization of space-time. Yet, how is it possible to locate a point and establish an instant without positing, either beforehand or simultaneously, a space and a time within which these can be established? This premise demonstrates one aspect of the relation between materialism and formalism:

Matter (in the scientific sense) is already in space and time. Thus matter represents the refusal to think away spatial and temporal characteristics and to arrive at the bare concept of an individual entity. It is this refusal which has caused the muddle of importing the mere procedure of thought into the fact of nature. The entity, bared of all characteristics except those of space and time, has acquired a physical status as the ultimate texture of nature; so that the course of nature is conceived as being merely the fortunes of matter in its adventure through space.[36]

The geometrical forms of space-time become the real and constitutive structures of matter. Ruyer provides a remarkable summary when he writes, "We now perceive the essence of materialism. It is a doctrine which takes a simple operative abstraction to be the supreme reality, the correspondence between two fields which substantiate, under the name of atoms of matter, the endpoint of relations."[37]

According to the interpretation given above, bifurcation necessarily entails the localization that completes it and provides it with its formal tools. The three premises that I have tried to outline form the axes from which this relation between bifurcation and localization draws its effectiveness. Whitehead's position is unambiguous: "I shall argue that among the primary elements of nature as apprehended in our immediate experience, there is no element whatever which possesses this character of simple location."[38]

The Reification of Abstractions

The idea that the notion of matter that follows from bifurcation is organized around a principle of simple location has some analogy with the thought of Bergson.[39] Whitehead was undoubtedly inspired by Bergson, to whom he paid homage on many occasions. In *The Concept of Nature* he writes, "I believe that in this doctrine I am in full accord with Bergson,"[40] and *Process and Reality* opens with the statement that Whitehead is "greatly indebted to Bergson, William James, and John Dewey. One of my preoccupations has been to rescue their type of thought from the charge of anti-intellectualism, which rightly or wrongly has been associated with it."[41] It is not a question of outlining all the elements of the influence of Bergson's thought, which would have to be linked to that of James, on Whitehead's philosophy. The problem is both more limited and more incisive than that of some kind of philosophical influence. It concerns the way of diagnosing the modern conception of nature and the conditions for going beyond this.

Therefore, I will take up only those elements of Bergson's thought that seem linked to, and able to clarify, Whitehead's conceptualization of localization, in order to outline both the similarities and differences that animate these two philosophical positions, and which represent two ways of resisting the bifurcation of nature.

In *Creative Evolution*, Bergson writes,

> Perfect spatiality would consist in a perfect externality of parts in their relation to one another, that is to say, in a complete reciprocal independence. Now, there is no material point that does not act on every other material point. [. . .] It is undeniable that there is no entirely isolated system, yet science finds means of cutting up the universe into systems relatively independent of each other, and commits no appreciable error in doing so.[42]

The independence of parts, and the possibility of science to define matter in terms of spatiality, correspond exactly to what Whitehead understands by "localization." Nevertheless, if the two terms—"localization" and "spatialization"—outline similar characteristics, they can be distinguished at a more general level, that of the relations that exist between abstractions and experience. To outline this, I will discuss how Bergson describes the function and status of science. Again in *Creative Evolution*, he explicitly poses the question "What is the essential object of science?": "It is to enlarge our influence over things. Science may be speculative in its form, disinterested in its immediate ends: in other words we may give it as long a credit as it wants. But, however long the day of reckoning may be put off, some time or other the payment must be made. It is always then, in short, practical utility that science has in view. Even when it launches into theory, it is bound to adapt its behaviour to the general form of practice."[43]

In this passage, Bergson clearly identifies science with practical activity. Asking the question "What is science?" therefore amounts to asking "How can knowledge act upon things?" Bergson clarifies his point: "Action, we have said, proceeds by leaps. To act is to readapt oneself. To know, that is to say, to foresee in order to act, is then to go from situation to situation, from arrangement to rearrangement."[44] And it is this practical orientation of science that is the foundation of the generalization of spatialization as a scientific interpretation imposed upon the world. Thus, "science may consider rearrangements that come closer and closer to each other; it may thus increase the number of moments that it isolates, but it always isolates moments."[45] The difference between classical science and modern science, between research that privileges certain places and times and research that demonstrates an indifference to specific places and times (all instants are equal), changes nothing about the essence of science: "Modern, like ancient, science proceeds according to the cinematographical method. It cannot do otherwise; all science is subject to this law."[46] It is at this point that Bergson is able to establish a link between common sense and science, through a general conception of the function of intelligence: "The science of matter proceeds like ordinary knowledge. It perfects this knowledge, increases its precision and its scope, but it works in the same direction and puts the same mechanism into play."[47] Spatialization is reduced to a natural inclination of intelligence, its vital dimension.

While Whitehead and Bergson agree on the importance of spatialization, nevertheless they part ways when it comes to determining its causes and consequences. "On the whole," Whitehead writes, "the history of philosophy supports Bergson's charge that the human intellect 'spatializes the universe'; that is to say, that it tends to ignore the fluency, and to analyse the world in terms of static categories. Indeed Bergson went further and conceived this tendency as an inherent necessity of the intellect. I do not believe this accusation; but I do hold that 'spatialization' is the shortest route to a clear-cut philosophy expressed in reasonably familiar language."[48]

Whitehead says no more on this. Nevertheless, it is possible to use this passage to bolster his critique. Their positions seem very close, and yet the difference is important and can be expressed in one word— exaggeration. At first sight, this is a strange way of rejecting Bergson. Yet, this is the latent core of Whitehead's position: he would have been prepared to follow Bergson in his analyses, in the way in which he describes spatialization, but he would have liked him to have slowed down the speed of his critique. The Bergsonian conception of spatialization is relevant, but his exaggeration raises it to a level where it becomes illegitimate and, more seriously, renders it incapable of the surpassing that it calls for.

What exactly is this exaggeration? Certainly, the history of philosophy (and one could add the history of science to Whitehead's remark) has confirmed Bergson's analysis, but nothing authorized him to make spatialization a necessity that is inherent to the intellect. For example, when Bergson states, in *The Creative Mind*, that "*our intelligence, when it follows its natural inclination, proceeds by solid perceptions on the one hand, and by stable conceptions on the other*. It starts from the immobile and conceives and expresses movement only in terms of immobility,"[49] he adds a dimension to spatialization that exceeds the framework in which it was established. From this there follow two consequences, which Whitehead rejects. First of all, by making spatialization a necessity of the intellect, Bergson is forced to place all the different ways of doing science under one general rubric. He recognizes fundamental differences between, for example, classical science and modern science, but, ultimately, these share the same approach. The diversity of methods, the divergences within the history of science, the multiplicity of models, and the tensions in the processes of experimentation seem to conjoin within the same underlying activity. It is the enormity of Bergson's diagnosis that comprises the exaggeration. The analysis of scientific activity, for Bergson, is possible only in terms of the extreme generality within which it is posed. As a result, and this is a problem that is even more important for Whitehead, the dramatization of the identification of spatialization with intelligence leaves little room for alternatives. Second, Bergson states that "*to philosophize means to reverse the normal direction of the workings of thought*,"[50] and he is obliged to look for the conditions of nonspatialized thought. Hence, the metaphysics to which he appeals necessarily takes on the appearance of a science "which claims to dispense with symbols."[51] The exaggeration that Whitehead denounces is the belief that science would be profoundly vitiated by a spatializing intelligence. Thus, Jean Wahl, seeking to develop Whitehead's remarks, writes, "There has been a confusion of science with the materialist conception with which it has too often been linked. Bergson and the Romantics have made of science a static and dogmatic conception; Einsteinian relativism and more recent theories would allow for an integration of what had been thought to escape science into a more supple science."[52] There is, however, no need to invoke new sciences, as Wahl does; scientific abstractions do not have a unique character that corresponds to a function that is linked to practical activity. Making such an assertion runs the risk of underestimating the transformative capacity of abstractions.

One of the functions that Whitehead gives to philosophy is as follows: "Philosophy is the criticism of abstractions which govern special modes of thought."[53] It would be completely wrong to think that by stating that the function of philosophy is to criticize abstractions, Whitehead is attempting to rescue experience from their grip, as if an experience without abstraction were possible. The term "criticism" that Whitehead uses in this passage, rather than referring to its usual oppositional sense, has more of a Kantian connotation: determining the limits of abstractions, the conditions of their action, and their effects in experience. It would be no exaggeration to see Whitehead's philosophy as one of the boldest attempts to give abstractions a fundamental role in experience. Abstractions are neither representations nor generalizations of empirical states of affairs but *constructions*, the "true weapons with which to control our thought of concrete fact."[54] It should be noted that the term "abstraction" already goes well beyond the logicomathematical model of abstractions and forms of substantialization in language with which it has been too often identified, notably by Bergson, thereby becoming the key to all interpretation of experience. Abstractions have their own constraints, their own modes of fabrication, their own ways of moving and acting. It is thus an inquiry into the mode of existence of abstractions and their function in the most concrete experiences (of which they are not simply formal reproductions), that is fundamental to the philosophy of Whitehead.

Whitehead never engages in a general denunciation of the notion of intelligence, but he does develop a critique of a specific scientific formalism, one that is constitutive of a physicalist materialism that has imposed itself during the last three centuries. It is against this that he offers another scheme of thought, another cosmology. While Whitehead agrees with Bergson that spatialization is central to all the difficulties of modern science with regard to thinking matter, space, the relations between entities, and so on, he nevertheless limits its scope to its influence during a specific period, and linked to specific abstractions. Thus, Whitehead's criticism is as much to do with spatialization considered as a theoretical model as it is to do with the attribution of this error to intelligence in general. It is in this sense that Whitehead's protestation in *Science and the Modern World* should be taken: "One main position in these lectures is a protest against the idea that the abstractions of science are irreformable and unalterable."[55] Similarly, Whitehead writes that the task of philosophy is not to reject abstractions but to demonstrate the limits of the abstractions that we have inherited, and the inconsistencies that they exhibit, and to reform our abstractions, where reform is still possible, or even to abandon them in favor of constructing new ones.

Going even further, it is not simple location that is the mistake, nor, moreover, the bifurcation of nature, for "by a process of constructive abstraction we can arrive at abstractions which are the simply-located bits of material, and at other abstractions which are the minds included in the scientific scheme."[56] The bifurcation of nature and localization are, above all, abstractive operations, tools that act as guides for experimentation upon nature. In this sense, they have a legitimate reality, and Whitehead comes to talk of them with great admiration: "We must note its astounding efficiency as a system of concepts for the organization of scientific research. In this respect, it is fully worthy of the genius of the century which produced it. It has held its own as the guiding principle of scientific studies ever since. It is still reigning."[57] The error lies not in what they have made possible but in the confusion of registers, in the reversal of orders. The paradoxes and the false excesses "only arise because we have mistaken our abstraction for concrete realities."[58]

The abstraction of the bifurcation of nature is one that is both produced and invented. Having found its efficacy in the operation that it enables, it now finds itself, through a strange procedure, reified; as if nature really were bifurcated in itself, as if the primary elements of experience really reflected the idea of simple location. The abstract has been confused with the concrete, effect with cause, the product of a process with its origin. In so far as "simplicity is the goal of our quest," Whitehead writes, "the guiding motto in the life of every natural philosopher should be, Seek simplicity and distrust it."[59] As long as the process of abstraction, the gestures and operations that were discussed earlier, remain active, and are assessed in terms of what they allow, there is no reason to question them. But, once this abstraction is reified, is taken to be the "real" foundation of a metaphysics, rather than a tool, this is when false problems take precedence over experience, doing "violence to that immediate experience which we express in our actions, our hopes, our sympathies, our purposes, and which we enjoy in spite of our lack of phrases for its verbal analysis."[60]

Whitehead calls the operation by which abstractions are reified the "fallacy of misplaced concreteness." Whitehead sums up the operation of reification that is at work in modern thought as follows: "My theory of the formation of the scientific doctrine of matter is that first philosophy illegitimately transformed the bare entity, which is simply an abstraction necessary for the method of thought, into the metaphysical substratum of these factors in nature which in various senses are assigned to entities as their attributes."[61]

A whole tranche of modern philosophy has strayed into bifurcation and localization, losing itself in their effects, notably that of dualism, without ever returning to the source of the operations that they claim to have gone beyond. Whitehead paints a picture that is undoubtedly incomplete but gives the general image of the kind of thought that was founded on bifurcation: "There are the dualists, who accept matter and mind as on an equal basis, and the two varieties of monists, those who put mind inside matter, and those who put matter inside mind."[62] The range of positions is clear, as they all share the same space, a common problem—one which accepts the primary existence of bifurcation but tries to reduce its effects while still confirming its importance. Thus, Whitehead writes, "the enormous success of the scientific abstractions, yielding on the one hand matter with its simple location in space and time, on the other hand mind, perceiving, suffering, reasoning, but not interfering, has foisted onto philosophy the task of accepting them as the most concrete rendering of fact."[63] Therefore, we do not have to choose between these alternatives, as they all confirm the gestures at the origin of this image of thought. It does not make sense simply to be in opposition to modern ontologies, as the operations from which they are derived remain implicit, and find their efficacy in their effacement. The modern experience of nature has consisted in trying to connect conjecture (real nature) to a dream (phenomenal nature).

Nature as Event

Bifurcation needs to be overcome. How is this to be achieved? All routes seem blocked. We are at a crossroads of different possibilities, but Whitehead's diagnosis of the emergence of the concept of nature within modernity seems to make any path forward suspect, to say the least. As has been seen, the alternatives are only superficial; the different ontologies that have been presented as ways to overcome bifurcation mask the operations and gestures upon which they rely. Through an analysis of the concepts of bifurcation and of localization, I have outlined the overriding interests at work in the construction of the concept of nature. These interests are essentially operative, practical, and derived from gestures of differentiation that aim to enable possible formalizations of nature, as well as ways of acting upon nature. We appear to be in a situation where everything is reversed: operations replace ontology, and abstraction replaces the concreteness of things, and the possibility of the knowledge of existence in itself.

However, in *The Concept of Nature*, Whitehead offers a way out of bifurcation, out of the strange correlation between abstract matter and illusory experience. It should be made clear straightaway that his solution comes at too high a price for it to be taken up. It requires that the concept of nature is instantiated on a basis that is entirely phenomenal and rejects any metaphysical stance. Whitehead subsequently changes his mind on this point, and this is the reason why, with regard to the critique of the cosmology of the moderns that runs through *The Concept of Nature*, it is only on the basis of his later works that it is possible to envisage a complete going-beyond of bifurcation. However, before turning to this metaphysical alternative to bifurcation, it is important to outline the solution that Whitehead had in mind at this stage, one that has notable similarities with phenomenology.[64] This will enable a better understanding of the requirements to which this foray into a phenomenological approach appeared to respond (although it should be noted that Whitehead was not aware of phenomenology as a philosophical movement as such), as he moves to his later metaphysics of nature, which in no way claims to invalidate his former theory but tries to circumscribe its limits. Several readers of Whitehead, such as Jean Wahl and Merleau-Ponty, have treated Whitehead's approach in *The Concept of Nature* as foundational for the rest of his philosophy. That is to say, they maintain that it is possible to draw from this book a philosophy of nature, one based on a phenomenal experience of nature. As a result, their readings of Whitehead are linked to a specific perspective that exaggerates the remit of *The Concept of Nature*. This is not an approach that will be followed here. Instead, the question of interest is that of knowing why a mathematician became an epistemologist and developed a general metaphysics. How is it that the solution offered in *The Concept of Nature*, based on a phenomenologization of the experience of nature, is both complete and partial, requiring the delimitation of a field of investigation while leaving in suspense those elements that are too insistent for Whitehead to hold back? The key phrase is "Nature is that which we observe in perception through the senses."[65]

This is primarily a methodological statement. It has nothing to do with any ontological assertion about nature itself, its qualities, its form, or the modalities of its existence. It only indicates a site, the primordial point of the experience of nature, and outlines the legitimate arena in which statements can be made about nature. Above all, this stance represents a decision through which Whitehead is able to establish the qualities of nature by making an appeal solely to immediate experience. The demand that Whitehead makes is that nothing is added that would overburden the significance of experience, but, especially, that nothing is subtracted from it—in a nutshell, "All we know of nature is in the same boat, to sink or swim together."[66] This is the moment of the setting out of a genuine method. Whitehead does not put it in exactly these terms, but implicitly his statements comprise a method that *The Concept of Nature* follows in the strictest possible way and that, once transformed and deployed in its most radical form, will become the proper method of speculative thought. Without doubt, the evolution of Whitehead's thought, the path toward a speculative approach, is linked to this method, which he never renounces: subtract nothing from experience. In his last work, *Modes of Thought*, Whitehead takes this up again and identifies it with a demand that is proper to philosophy in contrast, notably, to science: "Philosophy can exclude nothing."[67] This principle expresses a striking filiation with the philosophical movement that runs through the radial empiricism of William James, whose formulation is very close to Whitehead's method: "To be radical, an empiricism must neither admit into its constructions any element that is not directly experienced, nor exclude from them any element that is directly experienced."[68] It is this radical empiricism that is at work in *The Concept of Nature* and that compels Whitehead to focus on the perceptual experience of nature. It is this same empiricism that will later impel him to develop a general metaphysics whose speculative audacity Deleuze hailed at the conclusion of *Difference and Repetition*: "Philosophy has often been tempted to oppose notions of a quite different kind to categories, notions which are really open and which betray an empirical and pluralist sense of Ideas: 'existential' as against essential, percepts as against concepts, or indeed the list of empirico-ideal notions that we find in Whitehead, which makes *Process and Reality* one of the greatest books of modern philosophy."[69]

How, in *The Concept of Nature*, does this method transform the experience of nature? I will take as a starting point the method to which empiricism appeals. What is given to us directly in perception when we subtract nothing nor add any external element? Whitehead's response to this question is slightly disconcerting, as it opens up perception to a new level: "The immediate fact for awareness is the whole occurrence of nature. It is nature as an event present for sense-awareness, and essentially passing."[70] There are two distinct elements in this passage. The first is the "whole occurrence," that is to say the totality of nature that we witness from a perspective that is determined by the position of the body. We do not have clear access to nature in its totality, as this remains "veiled," but we have a vague experience of it. "We are aware of an event which is our bodily life, of an event which is the course of nature within this room, and of a vaguely perceived aggregate of other partial events."[71] Nature is perceived as dependent on perception, as we experience it only according to a perspective, and nature is also perceived as independent, as the vague perceptions of partial events are experienced as something beyond our current perception. The body, the perceived room, the building, provide a background of events that are not the actual object of perception but persist within it and open it up to aspects that are only vaguely perceived.

The second element is indicated toward the end of the paragraph. Whitehead ends by granting a particular quality to nature that he views as so utterly fundamental that he has no qualms in talking of its "essence." It is from this quality that all others in the experience of nature will be derived, as so many cases, or actualizations, of this first principle: passage. It is possible to talk here of an ultimate principle of the concept of nature, for nothing else is able to explain it except its relevance to those instances of perception that affirm its importance. Whitehead turns to Bergson once again to clarify his point: "I am in full accord with Bergson, though he uses 'time' for the fundamental fact which I call the 'passage of nature.'"[72] The task at hand is to take Bergson's notion of passage in its broadest sense. It points not only to a temporal transition, an evolution or a becoming, but also to a spatial change, a shifting of place or a movement. There is no reason to attribute any primacy to either of these dimensions. Any passage is directly or, to be precise, immediately temporal and spatial. Hence, as Wahl writes, "It could be said that the event which is the assassination of Caesar occupies space. The relationships of events to space and time are, in almost all respects, analogous. It is not that there are, on one side, objects in space and on the other, happenings in time; rather, there are happening-objects which are events."[73]

Passage is therefore an "event." This is the first time in Whitehead's work that the notion of event takes on such importance. From here on, from this decision to make event the primary characteristic of nature and the ultimate point of its experience, the whole of Whitehead's philosophy will become a vast inquiry into the notion of event. As Deleuze writes, in the chapter of *The Fold* dedicated to the philosophy of Whitehead,

With Whitehead's name there comes for the third time an echo of the question, *What is an event*? He takes up the radical critique of the attributive scheme, the great play of principles, the multiplication of categories, the conciliation of the universal and the individual, and the transformation of the concept into a subject: an entire hubris [. . .] an event does not just mean that "a man has been run over." The Great Pyramid is an event, and its duration for a period of one hour, thirty minutes, five minutes . . ., a passage of Nature, of God, or a view of God.[74]

Thus, the passage of nature is an event, as are the perspectives through which we experience it and the parts of it that we differentiate in our perception. All is event within perception.[75] I will provide some examples that will be grouped according to the aspects of events they demonstrate. There are three broad groups that can be identified through three statements:

1. "YESTERDAY A MAN WAS RUN OVER ON THE CHELSEA EMBANKMENT."[76] The idea of an accident or a particular occurrence is the most common characteristic of an event: something has happened. An accident, the unexpected overturning of a situation, the emergence of a reality that has seemingly broken with the causal chain to which it can be retrospectively linked, the greater or lesser rupture in the continuity of an experience—all fall under the idea of an event as an occurrence within nature. There is nothing surprising here. Whitehead is only taking up the usual conception of event and collecting various statements under the term "occurrence." However, by going a little deeper, a background of presuppositions can be found that are particularly acute in the "Chelsea" example. Where, exactly, is this idea of "occurrence" situated? Is it in the subject to whom something has happened and who preexisted this event? In this sense, is the evental element only an attribute? To clarify: In this statement, is the event situated in the man who was run over, or is it, rather, a broader reality, linking the witnesses, the victim, the driver, and perhaps the reports that populate the Chelsea embankment? Clearly something happened, but when we look more closely, it seems to be disengaged from any support, from

any subject to which it could be assigned or from which it emerges. Whitehead's stance, which simply follows the method that he has imposed on himself, is that we have no reason to reduce the event to something other than itself, that is, to what is given in immediate awareness. This change of perspective needs to be given its rightful place: in so far as the event is this occurrence, then it is the latter which gains real substantiality, and the man, the witnesses, the Chelsea embankment, and the narrator become its attributes. This is a crucial point. Whitehead wants to make the occurrence the basis of the event, its real substantiality, refusing to attribute anything else to it, except itself. There is more. The occurrence—"a man was run over"—unfolds within a multiplicity of spatial relations that become evident when we try to explain their meaning. It happened "adjacently to a passing barge in the river and the traffic in the Strand."[77] But this is also a temporal occurrence that is inserted within an infinite multiplicity of other past or contemporary occurrences. Thus, "The man was run over between your tea and your dinner"[78] expresses the temporal location of the occurrence within a constellation of others. This spatiotemporal relation of the occurrence, which situates it at the center of a collection of other events, is not an external context, as if time and space were only forms, receptacles, or axes within which events take place. Whitehead makes the relations between events the core from which time and space will gain their consistency.

2. "CLEOPATRA'S NEEDLE IS ON THE CHARING CROSS EMBANKMENT."[79] Granting the status of an event to the existence of this obelisk is a stance that, at first sight, seems to run counter to common sense. There is no notion of occurrence, passage, or temporal transition to be found here—notions that are clearly attributable to the events of the first category. What remains of the accidents, causal ruptures, and irruptions that form the substance of this first set of events? Looking more closely, the difference is not as marked as it might seem. It is possible to find the same elements but transposed to a new level. To make his case, Whitehead refers to a thought experiment, an imaginative change of perspective: "If an angel had made

the remark some hundreds of millions of years ago, the earth was not in existence, twenty millions of years ago there was no Thames, eighty years ago there was no Thames Embankment, and when I was a small boy Cleopatra's Needle was not there."[80] It all depends on the temporal perspective that is adopted. If we place ourselves within a particularly long time frame, the persistence of the obelisk becomes more ephemeral than it initially appeared. Additionally, when looked at in terms of a general overview, it is true that the obelisk seems not to change, but when we look more closely, if we immerse ourselves in its interior existence and analyze its constituent parts, we realize that beneath its apparent simplicity there is a multiplicity of modifications, variations, and interactions with its environment. Thus, a "physicist who looks on that part of the life of nature as a dance of electrons, will tell you that daily it has lost some molecules and gained others."[81] Whether we choose to look from a wider timescale or place ourselves within the miniscule variations that imperceptibly transform the obelisk, the result is the same: the continuity of the existence of the obelisk is an event that is not, in principle, so different from other occurrences within nature. The result, however, is important. If we agree with Whitehead, then all the "things" of our experience—material objects, physical objects, whether technical or biological—are events that manifest similar principles of passage and temporal transition. Whitehead's position displays a willingness to place all objects, in so far as they persist, within the domain of events. One instance of an event, an accident, or an occurrence does not directly display the idea of persistence but does presuppose it. In the case of the first example, it requires the persistence of the driver, the victim, the witnesses, of Charing Cross, in order for the accident as an irruption, a severing of the situation, to have a minimal level of reality. The accident unfolds against a backdrop of multiple persistences, in relation to which a difference is made. But what is persistence for Whitehead exactly? It refers to a notion of duration, to the maintaining of existence, to the very magnitude of being. As stated previously, if we place ourselves within these persistences, the deeper we delve, we find the multiplicity of little accidents, small changes, and transformations that, beneath the apparent stability and continuity of the obelisk, change it in each moment of its existence. A general rule can be drawn from this: persistence presupposes occurrence.[82] The maintaining of existence of the obelisk is nothing other than the repetition, the resumption, that Whitehead will later call the "historic route," of a series of occurrences, of small events, which are completely ephemeral from the perspective of its own existence.

3. "THERE ARE DARK LINES IN THE SOLAR SPECTRUM."[83] At first sight, this statement seems linked to the first two and appears to confirm them. It is tempting to see it as a renewed insistence on either the idea of occurrence (the fact that a dark line has irrupted in the solar spectrum) or the idea of persistence (the spectrum whose existence is implied by the dark lines). However, it is clear that Whitehead wants to draw out a new component of the event from this statement. It is not a question of talking about the existence of "dark lines" or of the "solar spectrum" but of setting out the relations between these two events. It has already been shown how, in a way, all events are essentially relational; thus, the impression remains that this statement says no more than the other two. In what way does setting these two events in relation to each other differ from the relational existence of other events? The specific element of this statement can be located in the *operation* of their putting-into-relation, through the introduction of a new dimension that is added to the events "solar spectrum" and "dark lines." Whitehead does not provide a definition, nevertheless I propose to call it "objective correlation." Whitehead's statement poses the following question: Two events being given, what correlation can be established? This activity is at the heart of those theories, principally scientific ones, which Whitehead believes this particular example of the solar spectrum highlights. That is to say, "If any event has the character of being an exhibition of the solar spectrum under certain assigned circumstances, it will also have the character of exhibiting dark lines in that spectrum."[84] Whitehead wants to situate theoretical, abstract, and operative elements in his theory of events. And this has important consequences. First, it breaks the

initial distinction between the events of nature and the manner in which they are represented—factual states and representations—and places them directly on the same level, on the same plane. All is laid horizontally on the plane of nature:[85] the ways in which we link events make up a part of experience itself; these manners are factors of existence that are as real as the persistence of the obelisk. It should be remembered that Whitehead lays great store by his method, to which there can be no exception. Theories are as much the immediate data of awareness as is the accident in Chelsea or the persistence of the obelisk. Stating that correlations are events, in and of themselves, leads Whitehead to the second consequence of his theory of event, namely, the idea that theories should be treated like all other events of nature. The question of the consequences of this relation between theories and events is left hanging at the time of the writing of *The Concept of Nature*. It will find its full expression in *Process and Reality* in the form of a theory of propositions, which will be returned to in the final chapter of this book. The important point, at the moment, is that in *The Concept of Nature* the scene is set. Scientific theories are events, marked by the same characteristics of occurrence, of persistence, of historic routes, of mobile connections. Thus the meaning of the event, as set out in this third statement, is that the "solar spectrum" event is connected to another event, "dark lines," by the intermediary of a third type of event, that of correlation. A completely different space of events is established, one that is linked to other events, and whose existence is founded in the articulation of these other events. What I have called *objective correlation* now becomes a new mode of existence of events, and is added to "*occurrence*" and "*persistence*." There is a complex economy within which these three components, drawn from *The Concept of Nature*, all presuppose each other. The accident unfolds against the backdrop of multiple persistences, which themselves are a series of irruptions that are maintained over the course of a common historic route; theories form a background of presuppositions which themselves exist only through their correlation with persistences and accidents that are already at work. Clearly, it would be wrong to make any of these components the basis from which the others gain their primary condition of existence. To reiterate: the method that Whitehead implicitly follows consists in exploring experience in terms of the immediate fact of the passage of nature as contained in awareness. In this respect, it is the intertwining of these components that forms the primary array of the plane of nature: the accident, the obelisk, and the dark lines correlated with the solar spectrum and the immediate fact.

But all events are composed of entities that are not, themselves, "evental." "As you are walking along the Embankment you suddenly look up and say, "'Hullo, there's the Needle.' In other words, you recognise it. You cannot recognise an event; because when it is gone, it is gone. You may observe another event of analogous character, but the actual chunk of the life of nature is inseparable from its unique occurrence."[86] Each event is a passage, inherently unique in its moment, different from all others, according to a rekindling of the principle of indiscernibles, but there are elements in all events that literally do not pass, elements which have neither spatial extension nor temporal thickness. We are having an experience each time we are able to say, "It is there, it is here again." This is the minimal, the most succinct, expression of the confirmation of the existence of an object. Something is here again. What exactly have we recognized? Variations of color, varying geometric forms, specific intensities of sound, particular sensa.

Whitehead, purely as a matter of convention, refers to these as "objects," knowing that their list is endless. As soon as something is recognized, it is an object. Whitehead's "realism" could be challenged by stating that all recognition is linked to habit, and that we only link the diverse qualities of events after we have reified them. If there is an experience of blue, it will always be through the repetition of particular experiences of "blue" that themselves are always different. But in what way are these cases of "blue" always different? If all events are different, if all experiences are changing, if each shade of blue is different from another, how can we recognize something? It is possible to go as far as one wants in this regression of explanation; in the end the question will always remain the same: How can we recognize something in what appears to be an original experience? Terms can be inexact, words can fail and correspondences run astray, but the impression remains that something has returned (even if it is the first time that we have experienced it), that one aspect of the event is analogous to another, that we have already experienced it under a different form.

Whitehead says nothing about how we could know "objects" in themselves, how we might know this "blue" or a pure geometric form, but, instead, he does talk of how we experience them *locally* on each occasion and how all knowledge is situated in relation to an event. Events are the occasions of the experience of objects. This is Leibniz's principle, taken up in a slightly different way, transposed to the level of nature, according to which "there are ideas and principles which do not reach us through the senses, and which we find in ourselves without having formed them, though the senses bring them to our awareness."[87] We can, therefore, know them only on "occasions," that is, according to a local dimension. Everything is reversed. There are no events without the objects to which they are linked and specified in a particular way. Conversely, we experience objects only in evental situations, on those occasions in which we recognize something that points beyond the experienced event. This is a strange mix, since its two elements have opposed qualities. The obelisk as an event is unique in its existence; it has its own time and space. From the perspective that we experience it, we recognize innumerable qualities within the obelisk, the multiple forms that constitute it, the colors, their variations and modulations. These "objects" are not simple projections from the mind onto nature, as this would return us once more to bifurcation, as if the colors, the sounds, and the forms belonged to us. Quite the opposite—it is the mind that finds it conditions of existence in, and is derived from, them. It is because there is repetition within nature—that which is recognizable— that the mind is able to make comparisons and connections.

Within *The Concept of Nature*, it seems that Whitehead already had the elements of a possible way of going beyond bifurcation. All appears coherent and consistent. Since bifurcation differentiates between abstract qualities and phenomenal qualities, it seems that there is a possible way of reuniting them through a theory of the events of nature, by placing these events within perceptual experience. This is not a matter of a historical analysis of the development of Whitehead's thought, of the development of an idea within his work. It signals a deeper problem, one that is much more important for the concerns of this book. If, as I have attempted to demonstrate, the theory of events relies on a method (taking only perceptual experience into account) and a premise (nature as a passage or an event of all events) does this, in itself, provide a systematic and coherent way of going beyond the modern bifurcation of nature? By choosing to place nature on a "phenomenal" plane, what must be given up and what needs to be excluded? What does the method that Whitehead follows in *The Concept of Nature* oblige him, despite everything, to deny?

To put it bluntly: the possibility of going beyond bifurcation was at this stage linked to a decision to exclude any metaphysical consideration of nature. Numerous ambiguities and misunderstandings in readings of the work of Whitehead are due to a lack of understanding of the stance that Whitehead took, and which he clarifies on several occasions: "I must repeat that we have nothing to do in these lectures with the ultimate character of reality."[88] He states that any deviation from this position would be disastrous, and puts his point dramatically: "The recourse to metaphysics is like throwing a match into the power magazine. It blows up the whole arena."[89] Whitehead's stance is not straightforward, and he recognizes that it places considerable limits on his enterprise. This is frustrating, as it continually points to a necessity beyond itself. In so far as the experience of nature as passage is both situated and autonomous in relation to perception, this inevitably leads to the question of the beings that compose nature. Whitehead is aware of this, and he recognizes that "it is difficult for a philosopher to realise that anyone really is confining his discussion within the limits that I have set before you. The boundary is set up just where he is beginning to get excited."[90] It seems as if the construction of the concept of nature on a phenomenal basis, and the theory of events that has already been outlined, forces those who follow this path to reject any metaphysical considerations. The method may well have been radical, as it goes beyond an investigation of nature in itself, and brackets all ontological and metaphysical questions. The question of the subject, and its relationship to nature, is only a heuristic one. This does not invalidate Whitehead's project, as it is principally a matter of setting out "the basis of a natural philosophy which is the necessary presupposition of a reorganised speculative physics."[91] Going beyond the bifurcation of nature would be a local affair, limited to the history of science and the construction of a new speculative physics. This would not involve taking any position on reality or on a nature that is independent of perception. This was the condition of the success of the theory of events: renounce any metaphysical position.

CHAPTER TWO

A Universal Mannerism

~~~~~~

The theory of events that Whitehead sets out in *The Concept of Nature* allows only for a localized going-beyond of bifurcation. This is why it is unsatisfactory. The decision to stick only with immediate perceptual experience and to reconstruct a concept of nature on this basis has its limits: it requires the rejection of any position on the real, the relations between events in themselves, the plurality of modes of existence in nature, even the sources of knowledge. Even more serious: it runs the risk of only being able to go beyond bifurcation by focusing on one of its branches, namely, secondary qualities. It should be noted that Whitehead does not later contradict the theory of events that he developed in *The Concept of Nature*, but recognizes that it needs to be deployed at a new level, as not just phenomenal but also genuinely metaphysical. It is now a matter of dealing fully with all those questions that *The Concept of Nature* refused to take up: What are the conditions of existence of events beyond perceptual experience? Where are the relations that animate them situated? How are these able to constitute the plurality of the orders of nature and mark themselves out within the domains of physics, biology, and anthropology?

I will start with a proposition that the following pages will attempt to give its full speculative scope. This proposition is first formulated by Whitehead in his magnum opus *Process and Reality*: "Apart from the experiences of subjects there is nothing, nothing, nothing, bare nothingness."[1] This is a rather strange statement, in both its style, so unusual for Whitehead, and its content. Without doubt, it is intended to be radical. Its emphatic character, compelling and repetitive, leads one to believe that when making this pronouncement Whitehead had the feeling that he was introducing a new thought, a tipping point in the field of contemporary philosophy. Why else would he have presented it in this particular way, if he had not felt that it expressed a rupture with those philosophical movements to which he himself had been attached and of which he had been one of the principal agents since the time of *Principia Mathematica*?

However, this proposition has not had the impact that Whitehead envisaged. Most readers of Whitehead, when they have lingered upon it, have paid little attention. How could it be otherwise? Does it not signal a return to a rather outdated philosophical question, the question of subjectivity? Everything in Whitehead's philosophy seems opposed to such a revival: his speculative and metaphysical approach clearly signposted in the first pages of *Process and Reality*, which has the subtitle *An Essay in Cosmology* and whose first chapter is titled "Speculative Philosophy"; the importance of the concept of process whose meanings go well beyond any notion of subjective change; the recurrent, insistent critique of all forms of substantialism (the importance of which has already been partly seen in the previous discussion of scientific materialism); and finally, the very function that Whitehead grants to philosophy, that of an "assemblage" of different modes of existence within nature. Given all this, how could he declare a return to the notion of subjectivity in his most radically antisubjectivist work? Perhaps, it could have become only a limited question, one that treats subjectivity as a particular domain of experience in nature. Thus, Whitehead would have been able to have left a place for subjectivity, alongside the classic questions of cosmology that are taken up within *Process and Reality*, such as the constitution of space-time, the difference between physical and biological existence, and the internal and external relations between the ultimate constituents of reality. This would have posed no problems to the overall coherence of Whitehead's avowedly cosmological project. But this is clearly not the case. The proposition goes much further, and those readers who are accustomed to the particularly technical style of *Process and Reality* will well know that he was not looking to grant such a place to subjectivity, despite all else, and at the risk of undermining the coherence of his system, but that this problem was inscribed within the cosmological ambition of his project. This has led to a false alternative: either the question of subjectivity is a local one, though the emphatic character of Whitehead's statement clearly does not lead in this direction, or it is to do with something more profound, something that bears upon the very dynamic of this new cosmology and, hence, should be ignored—but at what price?

As a result, the proposition remained dormant. In the following pages, I will try to grant it a more central position, making it a metaphysical hinge for subjects, and I will mobilize the principal concepts to be found in Whitehead's work in order to consolidate it. The reason that this task is important today is not simply to do with a point of interpretation of Whitehead. Although several important readers of Whitehead have been mentioned, this was not to point up their inadequacies but was an attempt to understand the uneasiness that has accompanied this proposition, in order to stress the fact that this proposition cannot be taken for granted. My aim is not to pass judgment on readings of Whitehead's work, nor is it to offer a better way of taking on his thought. My motivation lies elsewhere, as partially outlined in the previous chapter. If bifurcation affects all aspects of the cosmology of the moderns, an alternative will be coherent only if it redistributes all the elements of experience that have been divided and confined to overly specific and constricted domains. Thus, what would happen if primary and secondary qualities, far from being separated, were articulated differently and became the internal aspects of all existence? What experience of nature would we have if all secondary qualities, in the broadest sense—that is to say, colors, sounds, aesthetic tones, gradations of importance, values, ends—were all introduced, on an equal basis, within beings themselves? Does our contemporary experience not force us to quit a purely anthropological paradigm in order to elicit the centers of experience, manners of being, multiple relations that existents have with each other, and which make up a nature that has become essentially plural? What is important, following William

James, is being able to give sense to a nature composed "of personal lives (which may be of any grade of complication, and superhuman or infrahuman as well as human), variously cognitive of each other [. . .], genuinely evolving and changing by effort and trial, and by their interaction and cumulative achievements making up the world."[2] My interest in Whitehead's proposition, which will now be referred to as "the metaphysical principle of subjectivity," should be taken in this context. This proposition could become the first principle in the construction of a speculative scheme whose aim is to give sense to the multiplicity of manners of having an experience, a veritable panexperientialism.

The Metaphysical Principle of Subjectivity

Without doubt, we are, today, in a better position to understand the unease of more attentive readers of Whitehead's work regarding the proposition that we are discussing. The main impression, supported by the context of contemporary philosophy, is that the question of subjectivity necessarily refers, despite all due care being taken, to an anthropological subjectivity with which it has been necessary to break. This is the heart of the problem. Either the notion of subjectivity mobilizes categories such as intentionality, mind, and the capacity to represent, which link it to a theory of principally human faculties, and which cannot be the basis of a more general metaphysics; or it is emptied of all its features but therefore becomes an empty shell that can easily be dispensed with. The metaphysical principle of subjectivity must therefore respond to a double demand: to pertain to all beings, that is, not to exclude any of them, and, at the same time, to be coherent enough for it to make a genuine difference.

Whitehead grants a central component to the notion of subjectivity, one that is able to respond to this double demand: feeling. Before turning to the implications and transformations involved in this concept when it is taken up in a metaphysical context, I will first look at its current usage in order to draw out certain elements whose meaning will be clarified later on. Whitehead uses the word "feeling" as both a noun and a verb, and retains the ambiguity between these usages. Thus, he talks of "sensation," a general sense, a mood, or vague awareness of a situation, that is, the affective tonalities, the act or action by which something is properly felt.³ Whitehead retains the ambiguity of the word "feeling," as he wants to merge its two aspects. It would be a pure fiction to place sensations and impressions on one side and the manners and tonalities in which they are experienced on the other. When an animal "feels" a danger, when it is alert, can we really separate its individual impressions from the vague sense of dangerousness, of which all its surroundings become an expression? Does each impression not have its own particular hue, according to the general sense that accompanies the situation? But this more general sense has no real modality of its own if it is not linked to ongoing actions, to the "awareness" of other opportunities. Thus, even in its everyday usage, the two meanings of the word "feeling" come together: sense and impressions, the modalities of experience and the data that they convey.

Against all expectations, Whitehead locates the source of his conception of "feeling" in Descartes's *Metaphysical Meditations*: "The word 'feeling,' as used in these lectures [*Process and Reality*], is even more reminiscent of Descartes."⁴ For those who hope for a definitive end to, or at least a reduction of, the ambiguities that have been listed above, notably that of the overbearing attachment of the notion of subjectivity to an anthropological project, this reference is somewhat unwelcome. But we should not go too quickly. What exactly is the legacy that Whitehead draws on when he says that it all concerns the question of feeling? How did Descartes describe this notion of feeling? The passage in question is to be found in the second *Meditation* and is to do with appearances:

> I am the same who feels, that is to say, who perceives certain things, as by the organs of sense, since in truth I see light, I hear noise, I feel heat. But it will be said that these phenomena are false and that I am dreaming. Let it be so; still it is at least quite certain that it seems to me that I see light, that I hear noise and that I feel heat. That cannot be false; properly speaking it is what is in me called feeling [*sentire*]; and used in this precise sense that is no other thing than thinking.⁵

Whitehead provides only a brief commentary on this passage. He writes that "in Cartesian language, the essence of an actual entity [subject] consists solely in the fact that it is a prehending [feeling] thing."[6] I will now try to provide a possible reading of what Descartes is saying. Two things are worth noting in the context of this thinking about feelings. First, Descartes outlines the certainty of the act of feeling. All may well be illusory with regard to simple appearances or chimeras, but the act itself cannot be an illusion. It has a special status; at each moment this act affirms its own reality for itself, it arises in its own existence, independently of any position regarding the reality of the things that support it. The source of heat and the objects from which visual impressions emanate may well be illusory, pure fantasies or projections, but the act of feeling is incontestable, real for itself, it needs no other justification than its activity. Second, Descartes places feeling on an extremely broad plane: seeing light, hearing a sound, sensing heat, up to the final identification of feeling and thought. Whether it is an ambiguity within the text itself or not, Descartes identifies the act of feeling with thought itself. There is no doubt that Whitehead ultimately wants to take this relation further by highlighting the primacy of feeling over thinking, but the possibility of such an identification is already sufficiently clear for it to be remarked upon. The important point of this unexpected affiliation is that it allows Whitehead to establish feeling as a *constant* activity, which involves *all aspects* of a subject, and whose reality is in the *activity* itself.

This question must now be widened. Descartes's example, even if it highlights the fundamental features of feeling, is too limited. Indeed, it starts from a specific case, a very unusual and particular situation, that of a subject that is in full possession of its resources, capable of conscious reflection on the operations that stimulate it. It is a conscious subject that, in some way, manages to intensify the activities of feeling that stimulate it, such as the sensation of heat, in order to finally say that these feelings are "other than thinking." Is it possible to take up this example in less exceptional, less artificial situations, such as those of completely habitual behavior or where the question of what is being done has no direct relevance, as in the case of Dewey's walker who is only aware of walking when an obstacle arises? The question of feeling needs to be applied to all the features of the subject in Descartes's example, not only the experiences of the senses but also those of a dream, reflex actions, altered states of consciousness, so that all aspects of a subject are dependent on the logic of feeling. Furthermore, are directly equivalent experiences not to be found in realities of another order, microorganisms and primitive forms of life? If the artificial way in which Descartes presents his example is excluded, then is it not possible to take what he says of feeling and say it of all forms of life? This would constitute the first stage in the construction of what I will call a metaphysics of feeling: the generalization to all forms of life. "But animals, and even vegetables, in low forms of organism exhibit modes of behaviour directed towards self-preservation. There is every indication of a vague feeling of causal relationship with the external world, of some intensity, vaguely defined as to quality, and with some vague definition as to locality."[7]

The Cartesian subject distinguishes itself—especially from primitive forms of life—by the fact that it benefits from multiple centers of experience and a range of modes of perception (vision, hearing, touch) that might well be completely lacking in other living things. These enable the Cartesian subject to identify and locate, more or less clearly, the regions of its experience and, thus, to experience the "sensation of heat" in its hand. The difference between Descartes's thinker and microorganisms, as well as plants, is not the presence or absence of feelings (they all have these) but their different capacities to locate them and to modify them. The capacity to say "I feel heat in my hands," far from being primary evidence of life, is the product of an evolutionary history through which the faculties of experience have differentiated themselves. But, ultimately, the absence of distinct percepts in plants and microorganisms does not signal the absence of all feeling. It is not the feeling of this heat localized in a particular region of the body, but the "fuzzy" feeling of a causal relation with the surrounding environment. Whitehead gives several examples, trying to expand the realms of existence in which it is possible to identify analogies of feeling. "A flower turns to the light with much greater certainty than does a human being. . . . A dog anticipates the conformation of the immediate future to his [sic] present activity with the same certainty as a human being. When it comes to calculations and remote inferences, the dog fails. But the dog never acts as though the immediate future were irrelevant to the present."[8] Plants do not have percepts that enable them to state, to point, to show where, exactly, the light that causes their modifications is situated. However, there is undoubtedly a feeling of a change of environment involved as the plant turns toward the light. It is possible to say, with Descartes, that the source of the light may be only a total illusion, a chimera, nevertheless the activity of the feeling cannot be doubted, as it has its own reality. Something has been felt, even if in a very diffuse manner.

Against all odds, this passage from Descartes has enabled a thinking of feeling as a *constant activity that touches all aspects of the experience of a subject*. This is a crucial moment in the setting out of a metaphysics of feelings, as it allows for a determining of the space of existence as well as a widening of the boundaries within which Descartes's example was confined. Yet, even if the form of feeling has been clarified, this is not the case with regard to what comprises it. This raises a question: What, exactly, is this activity of feeling that has been described as being involved in both the Cartesian thinker and plants or microorganisms? The previous quotation from Whitehead gives us an indication. When he talks of a plant, a dog, or a human being, he locates a common activity under the various modes of experience that he calls a "sense of conformation." It is this that constitutes the primordial form of feeling. In the examples that Whitehead gives, it expresses a multiplicity of manners, of which the most important are the anticipation of a conformation of the future to the present, the adjustment of the present to the immediate past, and, more generally, the sense of the continuity of events. Santayana talks of "animal faith,"[9] which he finds at all levels of nature, a sort of minimal belief—it would almost be possible to say "physiological" if the term did not already connote too complex a mode of experience—in the fact that current events conform to the immediate past and that the future is not entirely disconnected from the prevailing course of nature. This sense of conformation might well appear abstract, but it has a real simplicity when situated in immediate forms of experience. As Whitehead writes at the end of the passage that was cited above, "The dog never acts as though the immediate future were irrelevant to the present."[10] This is the key aspect of a concrete instance of time that may, retrospectively, be sorted into dimensions such as past, present, and future but that actually overlap and form one movement whose irruptions are all linked to the sudden emergence of a reality that actively breaks through. This "sense of conformation," this primary aspect of feeling, is, above all, a sense of time: "Succession is not pure succession: it is the derivation of state from state, with the later state exhibiting conformity to the antecedent. Time in the concrete is the conformation of state to state, the later to the earlier; and the pure succession is an abstraction from the irreversible relationship of settled past to derivative present."[11]

When Whitehead talks of conformation, this clearly has nothing mechanistic about it; it is not at all deterministic with regard to the manner in which the present conforms to the past. In the examples that Whitehead gives, it is certainly not a matter of defining this living activity as the simple implementation of a program whose terms have been provided by previous events. When the plant turns toward the light, it is effectively conforming to the events of its immediate past, notably the rays that linger in its present experience, but neither the light nor the previous states of the plant unilaterally define the present action. It is the activity of conformation, an activity *in the present*, with which it is always necessary to start. It is this that defines what will be inherited, this local taking-up of the past, and the events that are anticipated.

This is the opposite of the position in which we suppose there to be distinct sequences that we then try to link up to provide some kind of continuity. Whitehead, like Bergson, establishes a genealogy of this reversal and considers such a view to be not an illusion but an exaggeration that, nevertheless, has its roots in a vital experience. The reversal of the characteristics of time, through which the discontinuity of abstract moments are replaced by the continuity of experience, by conformation, is not, as Bergson thought, the unique product of an intelligence that projects what are really its own characteristics onto nature. This inversion is more organic and primitive. It appears at specific moments in the organism, when "either some primitive functioning of the human organism is unusually heightened, or some considerable part of our habitual sense-perception is unusually enfeebled."[12]

Being as Capture

Feeling is a *present activity* of integrating the past. To clarify his point, Whitehead uses a technical term: prehension. There is no real difference in nature between the terms "feeling" and "prehend," but the latter outlines an important element of the activity of feeling. The term's primary origin is that of cognitive activity, an operation of knowledge, the act of "the intelligence seizing something." There is a prehension, in this primary sense, when the mind integrates, seizes, or makes its own a proposition, information about the world, a state of affairs, or a theory. The mind prehends, that is to say, it appropriates something for itself, a knowledge that was previously external to it. Only later is the term modified into diverse forms of the action of taking, while still retaining its cognitive status, notably, seizing an object by the hand; arresting a person, in the legal sense; or appropriating something. I will retain this general meaning of prehension: the capacity to take, to seize, or to capture something.

In the chapter devoted to Whitehead's philosophy in *The Fold*, Deleuze deploys the logic of prehension across all levels of existence: "Everything prehends its antecedents and its concomitants and, by degrees, prehends a world. The eye is a prehension of light. Living beings prehend water, soil, carbon, and salts. At a given moment the pyramid prehends Napoleon's soldiers (forty centuries are contemplating us), and inversely."[13]

The act of prehending is to be found everywhere, from primitive forms of plant life to Descartes's thinker, passing through the most insignificant perceptions. Past beings are taken, captured in a new existence, in a new act of feeling. It is as if each being had a double existence: one from its own perspective, its present activity, and that of its being taken up in later acts of feeling. Napoleon's soldiers, in their actions, appropriate the prior history that made them possible, and are appropriated by the world that comes after. It is in this sense that Whitehead invokes a genuine philosophy of possession,[14] of capture, taking up, prehensions. A subject is not a substance; it is a taking. Following Gabriel Tarde, it is possible to state that "possession is . . . the universal fact"[15] and that if philosophy "had been based on the verb

Have, many sterile debates and fruitless intellectual exertions would have been avoided,"[16] and that "for thousands of years, thinkers have catalogued the different ways of being and the different degrees of being, and have never thought to classify the different types and degrees of possession."[17]

We are now in a position to provide a fuller explanation of conformation. It has been shown how the reasons for the continuity of experience are to be found in actions-in-the-making and not in the realization of some mechanistic program, of which current actions would be only moments or expressions. Everything plays out in actions *in the present*. When it was stated, in the previous example, that the flower turns toward the light, it is because it has captured or integrated the previous act of the light. Nevertheless, some might want to argue that the light is the contemporary of the flower, and that its reaction occurs in parallel with the continuation of the ray of light. If such a position were to be adopted, it would make no sense to talk of the capture of something that has passed, rather, it would be better to regard this as the impact of present events. Similarly, with regard to vision, it would appear that it is solely concerned with things in the present. As a result, would it not be absurd to state that we see only things that have passed? This is not Whitehead's position, and we need to examine his position more closely.

It is always past events that are prehended, and even if this past might be infinitely close to the present act, the events that constitute the prehension are nevertheless prior to this present act. The flower prehends the ray of light that has just occurred, and we perceive an event that has just happened, but if this ray continues and if the event that we perceive extends for the length of our perceiving, then the continuity we observe is that of a repetition of acts of feeling. There are two parallel series of acts that are always out of phase: the series of the prehension of light and the series of the repetition of the ray of light. It is possible to say of any act of prehension that it is the capture of a prior event, and if this event endures it will be apprehended in a series of acts of feeling. Thus, the content of each act is provided by past acts, but these certainly do not define *how* they will be felt. That is part of a decision that is always in the present: the act of capturing hic et nunc.

It is possible to identify the metaphysical elements that are implied by feelings. I will start with a series of questions to which the examples already given, as well as the way in which feeling has been described, inevitably lead. When it was said that it is always past acts that are felt, prehended, or captured, how far into the past does this go? Is it a question of acts that form the immediate past of any feeling, or do they also involve, by degrees, a more distant past? Where are the limits? Are there only feelings in adjacent spaces, in neighboring acts, or do we need to make sense of feelings that have no contacts, no direct connections? Finally, from a metaphysical perspective, what is it that distinguishes acts that are important or significant, with regard to a specific feeling, from those that are trivial or inconsequential for the present act? Such questions could be extended infinitely, but they all come back to the same thing: what constitutes the act of feeling?

If nothing is added to what has already been set out, then the answer imposes itself: it is the entire antecedent universe that is captured in an act of feeling. Whitehead makes this the ultimate principle of his philosophy: "The many, which are the universe disjunctively, become the one actual occasion, which is the universe conjunctively"[18] or "The ultimate metaphysical principle is the advance from disjunction to conjunction, creating a novel entity other than the entities given in disjunction."[19] This principle should be taken in line with the vocabulary that has been set out in the preceding pages. Thus, each new act of feeling is the capture of the multiplicity (disjunctive plurality) of the previous acts that comprise the universe. Hence, in each act of feeling, it is the prior universe in totality that is felt. This might seem like an extravagant proposition, especially with regard to the examples given previously. It means that in an occasional act of thinking, in visual perception, in the conformation of a microorganism to the variations in its environment, it is always a matter of the universe in its totality. That which we think, perceive, or experience physiologically is always, from the viewpoint of the metaphysical principles implied here, an occasion on which the past universe in its entirety is contracted into one single act: *this* perception, *this* sight, *this* sensation. It is as if the universe ceaselessly contracts into a multiplicity of points that are so many centers of experience, perspectives of all that exists. It is important to note that these perspectives are not perspectives *on* the universe, but *of* the universe, immanent to it; they form its ultimate material. Thus, it is possible to say that they are vectors, "for they feel what is *there* and transform it into what is *here*."[20]

The metaphysical principle of subjectivity is therefore a way of re-vitalizing a monadological project. Following Leibniz, it is a matter of affirming that each act of feeling, or, in Leibniz's terms, a perception, is "like an entire world"[21] in which all previous acts are reflected. But, unlike Leibniz, there is no preestablished harmony that defines the acts and their relations, nor can any act of feeling exceed the limits that have been outlined, namely, that it is no more than a taking up of the past. Thus, when Leibniz writes that when "we carefully consider the connection of things we see the possibility of saying that there was always in the soul of Alexander marks of all that had happened to him,"[22] this is a general proposal that can certainly be situated at the heart of this metaphysics of feelings, but is quite different from that which Leibniz adds, namely, when he locates within this soul "evidences of all that would happen to him and traces even of everything which occurs in the universe, although God alone could recognize them all."[23] It is the impossibility of finding in a feeling anything but past acts that marks the difference between Whitehead's neo-monadological proposition and Leibniz's theory of expressions. The activity of feeling is always a taking of prior events, but tells no more beyond itself. As Deleuze puts it, in Whitehead "bifurcations, divergences of series, incompossibilities, and discord belong to the same motley world *that can no longer be included in expressive units*, but only made or undone according to the prehensive units and variable configurations or changing captures."[24]

In stating that all the antecedent universe, without exception, is feeling, that each event, no matter how insignificant it might first appear, leaves a trace that will mark all others, this theory of feeling seems to go too far. However, even this unprecedented broadening of scope is not enough, in Whitehead's eyes. Strangely, it still limits feeling too much. Saying that all the universe is feeling, is captured or possessed, according to a perspective, is not enough. It lacks a fundamental dimension that, as will be seen, will become the condition of the importance of these acts: the trace of all the possibilities that accompany feeling: "A feeling bears on itself the scars of its birth; it recollects as a subjective emotion its struggle for existence; it retains the impress of what it might have been, but is not. It is for this reason that what an actual entity has avoided as a datum for feeling may yet be an important part of its equipment. The actual cannot be reduced to mere matter of fact in divorce from the potential."[25]

What might have been, the choices made, and the selections that have taken place, are constitutive of feeling. Feeling carries with it all that "could have been," the eventualities that it had to avoid in its effective existence, all the alternatives that were presented to it. Hesitation in a particular action shows that possibilities are envisaged, ones which form so many routes of existence that are left in suspense, in favor of one specific route. Even if they are effectively excluded, they nonetheless remain determinants for the acts that are accomplished. Thus, all positive feeling, all capture, is always accompanied by a constellation of feelings of avoidance and denial, and rejections of possibilities, which amplify their importance. This is what Whitehead means when he writes, "The actual cannot be reduced to mere matter of fact in divorce from the potential." I will provide a fuller account of this in a later discussion of the status of speculative propositions.

Nevertheless, the importance of the possible worlds that are associated with each feeling should not be exaggerated. Contingency, hesitation in choosing, and the traces left by the rejection of a possibility have reality only for those acts that are actually realized. There is a real ontological primacy to the experience of actual feelings over potential feelings, of efficient acts (*engergeia*) over power (*dunamis*). Whitehead's proposition entails a genuine actualism. Although Whitehead does not directly lay claim to such a tradition, he intends to replace the principle of sufficient reason with another principle which lies at the centre of all explanations. He calls this the "ontological principle," and it appears to be an expression of the principle of all actualist thought: "The search for a reason is always the search for an actual fact which is the vehicle of the reason"[26] and "To search for a *reason* is to search for one or more actual entities."[27] This principle certainly does not negate realities such as the virtual, the possible, or abstraction itself, but it expresses the conditions of their existence. Each act must be "referable to one or more actual entities, because in separation from actual entities there is nothing, merely nonentity—'The rest is silence.'"[28] Thus all effective feeling carries the scar of the fact that it might not have taken place, and that this possibility does not hover in some ethereal world of abstractions but is inscribed, bodily, within that feeling.

The Subjectivity of Feelings

Feeling is the primary activity [operation] of all existence. Does granting such importance to feeling mean that we strayed from the initial aims of this book? What is left of the notion of subjectivity that was previously said to be central? Does it mean, as with those who were critiqued for their lack of interest in subjectivity, that this notion will be granted only a limited place, its existential relevance restricted, and it will be reduced to a specific domain of nature? Where is subjective experience itself to be situated in relation to feeling? Does "subject" now refer not only to the anthropological subject but to all forms of existence, as the subject designates anything than can be said to feel, to experience, to be affected by the world? Or, on the contrary, is feeling a primary activity that does not require any subject at all?

In order to respond to these questions, it is necessary to distinguish between two senses of the word "subject," ones that draw upon two distinct traditions in the history of philosophy: a subject can be thought of either as *subjectum* or as *superjacio*. It is important not to see these as opposed, nor to take up a position for or against either of them, nor to trace their respective limits. Each term demonstrates different aspects of the notion of subjectivity, aspects that could be seen as complementary in the metaphysics of feeling that is being offered here. Clearly, they are in opposition when confronted one with the other, but this opposition might well disappear if they are viewed as two distinct moments of feeling. I will argue that there are phases of feeling to which different aspects of subjectivity correspond. The characteristics associated with these two origins of the notion of the subject need to be outlined, as they express important dimensions of experience; they then need to be placed within the framework of the metaphysics of feeling.

I will start with the first sense. The subject first originates in the notion of *subjectum* that has imposed itself throughout modern philosophy. This term highlights the idea of being placed below, being thrown under something. The subject is thus thought of as that which, underneath all appearances, all varying attributes, changing impressions or superficial qualities, withholds itself and forms the support or basis from which these emanate. In his lectures on Nietzsche, Heidegger provides a description that might serve as a basis for identifying these qualities and reformulating them:

> The *subjectum*[29] is what is placed and thrown under in the *actus* and can then be joined by other things. In this joining, in the *accidens*, presencing-along-with in presence, that is, a manner of presencing, can no longer be heard. What underlies and has been placed under (*subjectum*) takes over the role of the ground upon which other things are placed so that what has been placed under can also be conceived as what stands under, and this is constant *before* everything.[30]

This question of *subjectum* needs to be placed within the metaphysics of feeling, as this is our present concern. To what experience, to what dimension of feeling, does this notion refer? If we follow Heidegger in the passage just cited, and translate it in terms of feeling, the *subjectum* is that withdrawn reality that forms the support, the constant base, and is the origin of feeling. The metaphysics of feeling, as set out so far, certainly does not fit with such a vision of the subject. Nevertheless, I will try to identify that which, in this statement regarding the subject as *subjectum*, is identifiable in experience in general. If this view of a subject that is in possession of its own feelings has markedly imposed itself on modern philosophy, it is because it evidently bears witness to certain fundamental traits of experience. It expresses the idea that all experience is focused, oriented toward a central subject from which expressive qualities emanate: affective tones, sounds, colors, tactile sensations, and so on. In so far as feelings seem to indicate a subject toward which they tend, then this subject might effectively appear to be the support from which they originate. But this appears only retrospectively. Only after the fact, when the activity of feeling has already taken place, can we attribute a source or a purpose beyond it. The order needs to be reversed or, rather, reestablished, and the relation of feeling and subject given its real genesis. The appearance of a support or a foundation of feeling, namely, that there is clearly a subject from which feelings derive, might appear to be a general and indisputable idea that various philosophies of the subject have tried to make their theoretical bedrock, but it is the *effect* of a process and not its goal. Let us return, once more, to Descartes, "Descartes in his own philosophy conceives the thinker as creating the occasional thought. The philosophy of organism [Whitehead's philosophy] inverts the order, and conceives the thought as a constituent operation in the creation of the occasional thinker. The thinker is the final end whereby there is the thought."[31]

This subject that is in full possession of itself and, hence, of its feelings (or, in Whitehead's example, of its thoughts), and that seems to be below its alterations and to act as a support for them, should not be considered as a primary reality but, quite the opposite, to be retrospective. The subject is the outcome of a "chain of experiences"[32] from which it becomes fully itself and acquires its own completeness. The subject appears at the moment that its feelings crystallize into a unified experience, a complex of feelings becomes a singular experience. Most of the time, a thought does not need to be tied to a subject, but if, retrospectively, we try to retrace the steps of its development, we can add a subject to it, when it is actually derivative.

This reversal can be generalized and assigned to all centers of experience within nature: an animal, for example, is composed of a multiplicity of centers of experience, "the various parts of its body,"[33] with their own feelings, their particular ways of being affected and of relating to the wider environment of their experience. But these multiple centers of experience, which are the parts of its body, are nonetheless linked to "one centre of experience"[34] that makes these multiple bodily centers communicate and form a complex unity, which lives and manifests itself as *this* feeling animal. Each center of experience of a body is a subject, in the sense that it expresses a plurality of feelings situated in one point of experience,[35] but the collection of these "centers of experience," in so far as they converge into a superior unity, also form a subject that is the animal, in that it comprises a complex unity of experiences. Ruyer, in a clear reference to Whitehead, uses the phrase "'superimposed' subjectivities"[36] to describe these entangled multiplicities. Thus, according to Ruyer, we should not hesitate to "grant to physical beings a subjectivity akin to that of a field of consciousness."[37] The articulation of these local subjectivities is the condition of the composition of the body. This will be addressed in more detail in the next chapter. For the moment, I would like to point out that the question of feelings can be posed at quite different levels of existence, but on each occasion it is a matter of a local unity of experience. A higher level of unity, a kind of dominant monad, is not always necessary, according to Whitehead. For example, "In the case of vegetables, we find bodily organizations which decisively lack any one centre of experience with a higher complexity either of expressions received or of inborn data."[38] There is certainly a multiplicity of small centers of experience, but these do not have to be subordinate to a higher center; this is why Whitehead states that a "vegetable is a democracy; an animal is dominated by one, or more centers of experience. But such domination is limited, very strictly limited. The expressions of the central leader are relevant to that leader's reception of data from the body."[39] Thus, this view of the subject as *subjectum* bears witness to an important element of the experience of feelings, but it needs to be seen as a consolidation of the latter,[40] as the endpoint of a process in which, step by step, a unified experience coalesces, into an experience of self: *this* portion of the body, *this* animal, *this* thinker.

Nevertheless, on its own, this view of the subject is not complete. It is liable to fall inexorably into a vicious circle. Whether the subject is situated as the origin of feeling, as in the classic conception, or at the end, as the outcome of a process of consolidation, as has been suggested here, it is as if there is a jump in the explanation that, at the same time, closes it off. If feeling were not already in some way subjective, or at least *capable of subjectivity*, how could it become? If subjective experience really were situated only at the end of a process, in its final phase, how could there be a passage from nonsubjective to subjective? This moment could be placed where one likes, at the start, the end, or the middle; but to talk of an amplification of the subjective dimension leaves us in the dark as to how this actually functions. If there is not already the germ of subjectivity at all levels of feeling, how could there be the question of a particular moment? It is here that Whitehead's adoption of another meaning of the notion of subject, taken from another tradition, makes its full force felt: the subject as *superjacio*. This could be translated in a variety of ways: "to throw above," or "to hurl toward." It no longer refers to a fully realized subject but rather to a tendency: "The aim is at that complex of feeling which is the enjoyment of those data in that way."[41] It is in the interior of feeling itself, in its forms, that this latent subjectivity is situated. It is, as Whitehead puts it, the manner in which feeling deploys itself. This subject is essentially a *manner*, the manner in which an experience is fashioned, the manner in which something is felt, the manner of witnessing. Each feeling is characterized by its *own manner*, a tonality that distinguishes it from all other feelings.[42] There is no need to postulate a subject that is both autonomous and the possessor of its experiences to realize that thoughts, that sensible impressions, already implement many particular ways of being linked to the data that their environments procure for them. This manner is the aim, the orientation wherein that which is felt is engaged or mobilized. Thus, it is possible to state, "The feelings are inseparable from the end at which they aim; and this end is the feeler. The feelings aim at the feeler, as their final cause."[43]

As stated previously, the two meanings of the term "subject"— *subjectum* and *superjacio*—are not opposed; instead, they can be taken up in a renewed thinking of the subject that is not limited to an exclusively anthropological context. If we start with the question of feelings, it becomes clear that there are two moments of a feeling that correspond to two subjective phases. First, in its initial stage, a feeling is mixed with that which is felt, that is, data, sensations, ideas, and general impressions. But a subjective form already inhabits this immanence of the feeling of data. Second, the feeling, in its first phase, may be almost indistinguishable from that which is felt, the manner, the focusing of data, is already the expression of a virtual subjectivity (*superjacio*), an immanent *style* of feeling. It is at the end of the activity that an experience of self emerges, which Whitehead calls *self-enjoyment*. It then becomes a subject in its own right (*subjectum*), the possessor of itself across the data from which it arises. Deleuze provides a summary that places Whitehead's project within a neo-Platonic lineage:

Self-enjoyment marks the way by which the subject is filled with itself and attains a richer and richer private life, when prehension is filled with its own data. This is a biblical—and, too, a neo-Platonic—notion that English empiricism carried to its highest degree (notably with Samuel Butler). The plant sings the glory of God, and while being filled all the more with itself it contemplates and intensely contracts the elements whence it proceeds. It feels in this prehension the *self-enjoyment* of its own being.[44]

In this way, Whitehead's gesture consists in making feelings the most fundamental characteristic of nature, rather than a supplement added onto it. The aesthetic becomes the site of all ontology; it is the plurality of manners of being, manners of doing, capacities to be affected, in a word, the modes of "feeling" that are at the center of a theory of the subjects of nature. This is not to revive the opposition between "reality" and "perception," "being," and "aesthetic value," in order to attempt to unify them, for nature can be directly envisaged as a multiplicity of centers of experience, each of which is directly expressive.

A Platonic Mannerism

There is no distinction between subject and manner. This statement, which has been arrived at while trying to remain as close as possible to the metaphysical principle of subjectivity, now raises new questions: Where, exactly, is the origin of these *manners of being*, which have been described as constitutive of all subjectivity, be it human or nonhuman, to be located? Are they only ever localized, only existing in a precise place, in a unique subject, or are they ubiquitous, finding themselves in a multiplicity of subjects that, therefore, have a common trait or quality? Are they transmitted, like a legacy that passes from one subject to another, or do they disappear with the subjects from which they seem, at first sight, to be derived?

These questions confront us with one of the most difficult and controversial aspects of Whitehead's philosophy. It has been seen that Whitehead does not subscribe to one school of thought but to a range of disparate affiliations, without losing coherence: the principal axes are empiricism, principally that of Locke; the pragmatism of James and Dewey; and the philosophy of Bergson. However, Whitehead also readily claims a heritage of a quite different nature: "The train of thought in these lectures [*Process and Reality*] is Platonic."[45] Without doubt, in Whitehead's eyes, the reference to Plato is not secondary or narrow but concerns the very principles of his system. He confirms this in numerous remarks, and leaves no doubt as to their importance: "If we had to render Plato's general point of view with the least changes made necessary by the intervening two thousand years of human experience in social organization, in aesthetic attainments, in science, and in religion, we should have to set about the construction of a philosophy of organism."[46]

Having chosen to situate Whitehead's philosophy within the perspective of a new theory of metaphysical subjects means that it is necessary to take a position with regard to the Platonic aspect of his thought, to identify its importance and current relevance. I will not look to diminish or reduce the extent of its application but, on the contrary, will follow this claiming of Plato as closely as possible, not out of a faithfulness to Whitehead's intentions or his texts, but because it is fundamental for the metaphysics of feeling. Taking up this aspect of Whitehead's thought is certainly not straightforward. How can Whitehead situate his project within both an empiricist lineage, under the marker of a superior or radical empiricism, and yet declare and take for granted, with no hint of provocation, that Platonism is one of his major reference points? Was it an unforgiveable ignorance of the oppositions, of the explicit and mutual rejections that these positions have made of each other? Was the relation to Platonism only a limited one, linked to a particular domain (for example, —abstract forms, logic, or mathematics), which could be added to the other domains of his philosophy, where the empiricist heritage is more appropriate? These questions take a very particular turn when they are asked from the perspective that has been set out in this book. We are looking to go beyond the modern bifurcation of nature by starting from a metaphysics of subjects, but if too fundamental a role is given to Platonism, is there not a risk of falling back into bifurcation through the introduction of a new dualism?

But what, exactly, is this Platonism that Whitehead claims? One will not find in the work of Whitehead any description, portrayal, or synthesis, as such, of the thought of Plato, as is also the case with the work of Bergson. The references are dispersed, and if they are to be given their due importance, it is necessary to take up these explicit references and draw out this strange Platonism. It will then be realized that this is a Platonism that is purified to the extreme, reduced to its simplest form, rid of "the systematic scheme of thought which scholars have doubtfully extracted from his writings."[47] Whitehead's Platonism aims to be the most authentic and direct, set out prior to the later interpretations to which it has been subjected. It is a Platonism reduced to its primary intuitions. Whitehead finds his basis in the *Timaeus*, the cornerstone from which he will develop the lines of inheritance that he envisages. He recognizes that "considered as a statement of scientific details . . . [it is] simply foolish,"[48] but nonetheless, it remains the case that a profound impetus runs through it, a cosmological idea that needs to be given its current context.

It may seem surprising that Whitehead formulates a purified Platonism, in that it appears to correspond to the most classical and the most familiar form of Platonism, in the general sense. Yet, what Whitehead essentially takes from it is the canonical difference between "first, the class of things which are unchanging, uncreated, and undying, which neither admit anything else into themselves from elsewhere nor enter anything else themselves, and which are imperceptible by sight or any of the other senses"[49] and, second, "the class of things that have the same names as the members of the first class and resemble them, but are perceptible, created, and in perpetual motion, since they come into existence in a particular place and subsequently pass away from there."[50] It is a matter of rendering this Platonic dualism in its initial state, without any unnecessary ornamentation or complex elaboration. Nothing should be added to this difference. The Platonism in question is clearly that of a distinction between two realms of being: those that "are unchanging, uncreated, and undying" and those that become. It is a matter of intensifying this difference to its maximal point. The hiatus between two realms of beings rules out any relation of resemblance or belonging. It is a matter of taking literally the idea developed in the

Timaeus, according to which the beings of the first order are inaccessible to "any of the other senses," separated from all sense experience. Whitehead calls these "eternal objects. In order to understand the contemporary importance of Platonism, it is this question of "eternal objects" that needs to be sought, as it is they that justify this lineage: "I use the phrase 'eternal object' for what . . . I have termed a 'Platonic form.' Any entity whose conceptual recognition does not involve a necessary reference to any definite actual entities [subjects] of the temporal world is called an 'eternal object.'"[51]

There are two stages to Whitehead's elaboration of the concept of "eternal objects." First, he establishes a primordial and ontological opposition between "eternal objects" and "actual entities." The notion of actual entity was met with previously, in the discussion of the question of feelings arising from Descartes's example. It is a notion that is absolutely central to Whitehead's speculative work, but to avoid the unnecessary proliferation of neologisms and technical distinctions, I will not provide a definition but will stick to the general sense that Whitehead gives to this term, namely, that of an existing subject. It is possible to state, using the terminology that has been developed up to this point, that anything that is not an effective feeling, a taking, a capture, an act of becoming is, therefore, an eternal object. Whitehead's procedure of defining "eternal objects" through an opposition appears to be appropriate. However, it presents a major difficulty. Indeed, the contrast is radical and allows for no accommodation: what exists is either an "eternal object" or a subject. Whitehead's proposition may have the appearance of a simple distinction, but it constitutes a bold decision. It literally excludes these objects from any relationship of belonging to ordinary subjects. They seem to float in a parallel world, without any "necessary reference to any definite actual entities," that is to say, to an everyday effective reality. But, have the previous pages not insisted, indeed, gone so far as to make it a metaphysical principle, that "apart from the experiences of subjects, there is nothing"? How then, is it possible to understand the status of these "eternal objects" if they are established in opposition to subjects? If, at this point, they are seen as opposed to that which forms the condition and basis of all existence, are they not reduced to nothing? This is not simply a matter of Whitehead's methodological stance. If it were, then it would be possible to limit the problem by stating that his method was not fully adequate, as it posits a separation at this point, when the rest of Whitehead's scheme denies any such thing. The problem is even more fundamental than this, as it concerns the very status of "eternal objects." Indeed, Whitehead confirms this duality of existence, leaving no doubt as to the difficulty of the problem that it poses: "The fundamental types of entities are actual entities, and eternal objects; and . . . the other types of entities only express how all entities of the two fundamental types are in community with each other, in the actual world."[52]

I stated previously that I wanted to follow the metaphysical principle of subjectivity as closely and as literally as possible, and not to pose anything as existing beyond subjects, but we are now confronted with a notion that totally contradicts this. There is another type of entities that are just as fundamental as subjects, which do not arise from them, which are certainly not derivative expressions of them, but which have a status in existence that is equal to them. These difficulties are neither accidental nor secondary; they are, as will be seen, a part of the instauration of "eternal objects."[53]

The second stage of Whitehead's elaboration of eternal objects is that, since an opposition has been set up between "eternal objects" and subjects, it is now possible to use this to identify some examples of the former. The difficulty with such an exposition comes from the fact that "eternal objects" can never be traced, in their changes of form or in generalizations of empirical data, and cannot be dealt with in themselves, in their pure form. We can indicate them only through a concrete example. Returning to Cleopatra's Needle, it was explained how this is an event that appears inalterable, at the level of our perception. But, by changing scale, either by inserting ourselves within its most fundamental constituents or, alternatively, by locating the Needle in the breadth of a history that it inhabits, including where it was created and how it has been modified over the centuries, we can certainly come to see the Needle as a singular event, caught in a becoming that is unique when compared to any other. Each event is singular, each moment is particular, nevertheless we never stop recognizing something within events: "As you are walking along the Embankment you suddenly look up and say, 'Hullo, there's the Needle.' In other words, you recognize it."[54] That which is recognized is not the change that affects the Needle, nor its singularity, but the entities that compose it: its particular color, its geometrical form, its particular texture, all those elements that persist in experience as being "here again" and that make the Needle comparable to thousands of other experiences, each equally singular in their effective existence. The experience of the Needle indicates those factors in its existence that repeat themselves, that are transposed from one existence to another, located in distinct moments. We never have an experience of a color in itself, nor a given geometric form, a pure sound, only their "ingression" in particular events: this variation at this moment and this place. Thus, it should be said of a color that it is eternal: "It haunts time like a spirit. It comes and goes. But where it comes, it is the same colour. It neither survives nor does it live. It appears when it is wanted."[55] We then see emerge categories and classes of eternal objects that can be found spread throughout the work of Whitehead: "sensa" such as "green" and "blue," but also shades of color; universals of quality; "sensa" functioning as qualities of emotion; qualities of form and intensity; the objects of objective space, such as mathematical forms; "patterns" and "relations."[56]

How can we account for these "eternal objects" in terms of a theory of subjects? Why is it so important to grant them a real status and to follow Whitehead when he says that the movement of his thought is Platonic? What place can they occupy in the metaphysical principle of subjectivity? The question with which we have been confronted until now is that of the *manner* in which a subject prehends the anterior world, *how* it captures it, integrates it, and constitutes itself via this prehension. As has already been stated, this manner is at the heart of subjective existence. But where does it come from? What is its origin and its source? It is tempting to reply by stating that the manner in which a subject inherits the anterior world derives from this anterior world since this is composed of nothing other than subjects themselves. At each "moment," the universe contracts into a multiplicity of points of perspective that are these new subjectivities, as has been discussed throughout this book. The process continues to infinity: each new subjectivity adds itself to the infinite multiplicity of the others in order to form the material from which a new subjectivity will be forged. But, if the *manner* in which this new subjectivity is derived comes entirely from the past that it inherits, where does the novelty come from? Thus, the introduction of eternal objects presents us with two clear alternatives. Either the manner in which a subject inherits the past is entirely defined by this past, that is to say, by other subjects, and, in this way, the universe repeats itself indefinitely, transferring given forms of existence from subject to subject without addition or subtraction. Or we need to admit that the *manner* does not derive from the past but is a condition of novelty beyond any inheritance and is therefore independent of subjects. I want to argue that eternal objects are, against all expectations, the conditions of this novelty. This is in full agreement with Deleuze when he makes "eternal objects" pure virtualities that come to define the novelty that they carry within events. What follows is a long quotation from *The Fold* in which Deleuze synthesizes all the relations between subjects—in terms of Leibniz's monads—as prehensions and virtualities, and explains these through the example of there being a concert tonight:

It is the event. Vibrations of sound disperse, periodic movements go through space with their harmonics or submultiples. The sounds have inner qualities of height, intensity, and timbre. The sources of the sounds, instrumental or vocal, are not content only to send the sounds out: each one perceives its own, and perceives the others while perceiving its own. These are active prehensions that are expressed among each other, or else prehensions that are prehending each other [. . .]. The origins of the sounds are monads or prehensions that are filled with joy in themselves, with an intense satisfaction, as they fill up with their perceptions and move from one perception to another. And the notes of the scale are eternal objects, pure Virtualities that are actualized in the origins, but also pure Possibilities that are attained in vibrations or flux.[57]

Thus, eternal objects become the fundamental condition of novelty, "their eternity is not opposed to creativity."[58] This is the full meaning of a cosmological mannerism: manners are not derived from anything, but they never cease to vary according to the local conditions of existence. The subject does not project onto nature, onto its experience, the manners that it will make its own, on the contrary, it is the local manners of prehending, of capturing and integrating, that form the conditions of individuation for an experiencing subject. Manners are therefore immanent to novelty, they are required for the production of a new subject.

But, if eternal objects are not derived from subjects, is there not a risk that by reversing the poles of the argument, the ontological importance of subjects is reduced as their particularity is located within eternal objects? In the more classical terms of metaphysics: if the potential—eternal objects—cannot be explained by the actual—the subject—are we not inevitably led by what Whitehead has set out, to explain the actual as arising from the potential? Potential, which Whitehead says is eternal, changeless, and with no origin, risks becoming a form, a principle of individuation, from which the actual will be derived. It is this issue, I would argue, that led Whitehead to criticize an approach that he considers to have been derived from Platonism: the theory of participation. He sees in it the temptation, which runs through Greek philosophy, to give to mathematics a scope that exceeds what might legitimately be expected. "Plato in the earlier period of his thought, deceived by the beauty of mathematics intelligible in unchanging perfection, conceived of a super-world of ideas, for ever perfect and for ever interwoven. In this latest phase he sometimes repudiates the notion, though he never consistently banishes it from his thought."[59]

The Platonic model of participation is not wrong, as such, and certainly remains a relevant way of explaining certain realities, but its metaphysical generalization is inappropriate, according to Whitehead. This is a criticism that is often to be found in his writing: a method associated to a particular domain of experience, such as the model of participation, and, more generally, the method of deduction, cannot have their relevance generalized and they cannot be transposed, as such, to other domains. It is in this confusion of which methods are appropriate for mathematics and which for philosophy that Whitehead locates the exaggeration involved in the importation of the model of participation, and the risk that accompanies constructing an ontology on this basis: "The primary method of mathematics is deduction; the primary method of philosophy is descriptive generalization. Under the influence of mathematics, deduction has been foisted onto philosophy as its standard method, instead of taking its true place as an essential auxiliary mode of verification whereby to test the scope of generalities."[60]

This is why Whitehead counters the model of participation with what he calls ingression: "The term 'ingression' refers to the particular mode in which the potentiality of an eternal object is realized in a particular actual entity, contributing to the definiteness of that actual entity."[61] Ingression is the process by which an "eternal object" is actualized within a new subject. It is not possible to think beyond the existing world, which is already composed of other subjects that determine the fields of possibility, and, hence, the actualization of this eternal object rather than another. Eternal objects are neutral with regard to the subjects in which they are actualized: "An eternal object is always a potentiality for actual entities; but in itself, as conceptually felt, it is neutral as to the fact of its physical ingression in any particular actual entity of the temporal world. 'Potentiality' is the correlative of 'givenness.' The meaning of 'givenness' is that what is 'given' might not have been 'given'; and that what is not 'given' might have been 'given.'"[62]

As opposed to participation, ingression is a genuine inversion, for it highlights the dependence of "eternal objects" on the world in its immanent process. These eternal objects neither account for the world nor do they provide its reasons, on the contrary, it is the world and its existents that solicit what is relevant and what is possible with regard to the state of the world in which they find themselves. It is as if the universe, in its creative advance, never ceases to create new constraints, which are the existents themselves, canalizing how they inherit what is possible, in a new way. If eternal objects did not have a formal existence and if they were not solicited by the world in which their local incarnations continuously vary, then subjects would be only mechanical repetitions. It is here that the essential demand of empiricism that runs throughout Whitehead's metaphysics is to be found: "Eternal objects [...] tell us nothing about their ingression in experience. In order to see them, there is only one thing to do: adventure in the domain of experience."[63]

Eternal objects, these manners of feeling, raise new questions: How does one manner of feeling transfer from one act to another? If all acts are different, new in their own way, and cannot be compared one with another, how is it possible to explain the persistence of a being over a longer or shorter period of time? If the universe is never twice the same, if creativity and the production of novelty are radical, how is it that we can have experiences of different orders within nature, of duration and persistence? In short, how does an eternal object or, more accurately, a complex of eternal objects, transfer from one moment of existence of an entity to another?

The Transmission of Feelings

Up to this point, the instauration of a metaphysics of feelings has necessitated an intensification of the individual dimension of the act of feeling: this particular *manner* of capture, at this moment. The examples that have been provided—a microorganism, a plant, an animal on alert, or even Descartes's thinker—cannot be reduced to simple acts. An animal's slightest sensation of the environment, in its most spontaneous bodily movement, or the most ephemeral thought, are never only simple and unique acts. Thus, when Whitehead writes that a "flower turns to the light with much greater certainty than does a human being," this should be understood as an intertwined multiplicity of acts of feeling—a genuine democracy—in which all are interconnected. Looking from the outside, it may seem that a more or less simple, although slow, action has taken place: the flower has turned toward the light. But a change of perspective, through the use of imagination or via technical means, can place us within this apparently simple act and enable us to see that it encompasses a multiplicity of small actions in each of the parts that compose the flower, of transfers, of transmissions from one moment to another throughout the duration that forms the specific time of this movement. Can the same not be said of the persistence of Cleopatra's Needle over centuries or of a flash of thought? Are these not also multiplicities, entanglements of acts of feeling that appear simple and homogenous from the outside? Is it not better to say, with Butler, that "each individual may be manifold in the sense of being compounded of a vast number of subordinate individuals which have their separate lives within him, with their hopes, and fears, and intrigues being born and dying within us, many generations of them during our single lifetime."[64]

I will refer to these collective existences, these arrangements (*agencements*) or articulations of feelings, as "societies." Whitehead's description of the life of a man takes up these ideas:

> The life of man is a historic route of actual occasions which in a marked degree [...] inherit from each other. That set of occasions, dating from his first acquirement of the Greek language and including all those occasions up to his loss of any adequate knowledge of that language, constitutes a society in reference to knowledge of the Greek language. Such knowledge is a common characteristic inherited from occasion to occasion along the historic route.[65]

In this example, Whitehead deploys a fundamental notion—that of "historic route." The life of man is a historic route in which acts of feeling succeed each other, forming a long and uninterrupted chain of transmissions and reprises. Each act takes up the acts that came before and transmits to those that follow. Whitehead describes a somewhat mundane aspect of the existence of this life, namely, knowledge of a language, such as Greek, in order to demonstrate that this historic route does not consist of one dimension, of one movement. Indeed, what would the life of man be if it were composed only of a simple succession of purely biological or bodily acts? Would it really be possible to envisage a life without granting it dimensions of a different order, such as learning a language, with its first steps, its developments and intensifications, its own manners of existing, up to the final moment when the language is forgotten? Does this learning, with its expectations, its hopes and failures, not also constitute a genuine history, a historic route that, in numerous ways, seems to live a life that is different and parallel to other dimensions of the existence of man? If this is allowed for the knowledge of a language, then how can it be denied for other dimensions of man's existence? Is not the life of each organ also a historic route that could have its own biography, similar to that of the knowledge of Greek? This life has become much more complex.

Clearly, it is made up of acts of feeling, but these range in multiple directions, forming many trajectories that might, at first sight, appear independent.

Nevertheless, it is always a matter of *a* life, of the *same* person. These historic routes can be unfolded to infinity, multiplying the perspectives in which they are engaged, showing that the times that compose them are plural, and it would be in vain to try to submit them to a common form. At the same time, it is impossible to escape the impression that this is a matter of one continuous reality. Does such an idea come from the illusion of a representation that projects its own categories onto the real and only finds what it has put there? Or, on the contrary, is it the affirmation of a fundamental dimension—identity—that the plurality of aspects of existence mask without being able to completely erase? The question of the "historic routes" of feelings, of the social organizations that are to be found at all levels of existence, does not mean that we have to choose between these two options. That it is a matter of the *same* life need not be reduced to any simple model of representation. This experience of the same and of unity genuinely expresses something that is real. But it does not entail the need to postulate a form of substantialism from which acts of feeling that compose this life would be derived. Beyond the acts of feeling, there is nothing. Yet identity is real. Whitehead clarifies what he means as follows: "A more important character of order would have been that complex character in virtue of which a man is considered to be the same enduring person from birth to death. Also in this instance the members of the society are arranged in a serial order by their genetic relations."[66]

It is the historic route that is the identity of this person. The history of the acts that compose this life do not determine the context in which it is deployed; it forms the most fundamental substance within it. This history is that of the manner in which one act follows another, inheriting it, and bequeathing its own legacy to those that follow. In this way it establishes the "genetic relations" or the individuation of these acts. Of course, no act of feeling can provide the reason for being inherited in one manner rather than another; inheritance is entirely free. However, the fact that it has occurred, that it was this act rather than another, means that the route in which it is engaged takes a specific turn. Thus, it is possible to say that such acts canalize becoming.[67] For example, an alert animal may not be in the immediate presence of a predator. Nevertheless, it feels a vague and unsettling presence as indicated by the signals of its environment. Evidently, its present action, its current attention, follow from past impressions, such as an unusual noise, an odor, or the sudden movement of other animals. It might move toward or away from that which seems to be the source of this danger. Whatever decision is made, each new act will take up the inheritance of this history to which it conforms, without this being in any way a mechanical repetition. The key point is that this account has not involved the positing of the existence of memory, of a mind or of habit, in order to establish the connection between these heterogeneous acts. It is within the act itself, in its deepest reality, its very constitution, that this history is established. It is as if each act is a memory that replays the entire history from which it emerges. This example can be taken further. The fear that an animal manifests in the particular moment that it senses danger is not reducible to a collection of sensations or perceptions. These realities could have been experienced very differently by another living being, with other affective modalities, such as empathy, sadness, or curiosity. The fear is nowhere, and yet it affects each action. It is only by pure convention that we say that an animal *has* a fear, as it is clear that the fear is in each of its actions and, more often than not, has taken possession of the acts before the animal is aware of it. We should say, rather, that the animal is possessed by fear and this possession is not something general, as it is situated in particular acts. Each action is inhabited by a modality of fear. It is the particular *manner* in which the past is integrated. It is within each act. It arises from nothing, although everything in this particular history, in this historic route of the alert animal, becomes the occasion of the existence of this fear. These characteristics of fear—the fact that it has no particular origin, that it is to be found in a multiplicity of acts of feeling, in distinct moments and places, that it displays a *manner*—remind us of the strange form of Platonism that was discussed earlier. Whitehead was always very careful in his use of examples, especially those regarding eternal objects, but one way of thinking about them would be to see them as this inheritance of fear from act to act along a historic route.

Hence, that which is transferred from one act to another is not only the content of the act but the conditions by which a certain affective tonality (eternal objects) ingress into a particular situation. While it always varies, intensifies, or, on the contrary, dissipates, fear is transmitted from act to act, forming the history of this particular route, which is the concern that has appeared in the life of this animal. To be precise, it is not so much fear that is transmitted as the conditions that enable fear's appearance.

Nevertheless, even if the identity of a society is to be found in the historic route that makes it exist, in the history of the acts that are taken up and transferred, a society is not isolated. The animal on alert responds to solicitations that come from everywhere and that intrude on each part of its being; the plant prehends the light and thereby demonstrates its attachment to the variations of its environment; even Cleopatra's Needle is continuously modified by its being affected by concomitant events.

A milieu is always a theatre of intense activity such as the "Castle Rock at Edinburgh," which exists "from moment to moment, and from century to century, by reason of the decision effected by its own historic route of antecedent occasions,"[68] continues, changes, and finally disappears. These examples, and the logic of feelings, demonstrate that a milieu is never a simple spatial framework in which actions unfold, or in which events gain corporeality. The fact that two individuals are spatially proximate does not guarantee that they share the same milieu. The entanglement of societies is such that the same spaces can imbricate different modes of existence, forms of experience, and levels, which do not necessarily meet. Following Gilbert Simondon, it is better to talk of "an associated milieu," to indicate the deep attachment and vital interest that an individual has to and with its environment.[69]

The doctrine that every society requires a wider social environment leads to the distinction that a society may be more or less "stabilized" in reference to certain sorts of changes in that environment. A society is "stabilized" in reference to a species of change when it can persist through an environment whose relevant parts exhibit that sort of change. If the society would cease to persist through an environment with that sort of heterogeneity, then the society is in that respect "unstable."[70]

It is in light of this deeply pragmatic question, regarding the difference between the stability and instability of societies, that it is possible to establish the emergence of the differences between "physical" and "living" societies. The problem of the distinction between the physical and the vital clearly goes well beyond the framework of this book. In large part, this distinction is a legacy of the bifurcation of nature; for allocating beings according to whether they manifest more physical or more living elements usually involves a new form of reductionism: either physicalist or vitalist. This is a similar gesture to that of bifurcation, now deployed at a new level. This gesture, which consists in extracting the essential qualities of beings, which are for the most part constructed, in order to set them in opposition to purely phenomenal, secondary qualities, now gains a new level of effectiveness. It is possible to use the relations between societies and their environments, as just discussed, to offer a change of perspective. Rather than start from a purely hypothetical division between those beings that principally demonstrate either physical or vital characteristics, in order to then establish connections between them, or to reduce one into the other, it is more accurate to envisage the effects of distinct responses to variations in the environment. What alternative view of the differences between physical and vital forms of existence would emerge if they were seen as different ways or manners of relating to similar changes?

A change of environment could give rise to at least two possible responses: indifference and transformation. I will start with the first. Indifference characterizes "material" or "physical" bodies. "These material bodies belong to the lowest grade of structured societies which are obvious to our gross apprehensions. They comprise societies of various types of complexity: crystals, rocks, planets, and suns. Such bodies are easily the most long-lived of the structured societies known to us, capable of being traced through their individual life-histories."[71]

Clearly, all societies are continually affected by their environment— exchanges, destructions, metamorphoses—but physical societies are characterized by their capacity for indifference. Everything affects them.

They are at least as subject to alterations, most often imperceptible, as "living societies," but they seem able to ignore them. That which allows them to maintain a certain stability, that which is the condition of their survival, is that they demonstrate *"grossness."* Whitehead uses this phrase humorously, in order to indicate a particular aspect of this response to changes. This somewhat unusual term can perhaps be understood as expressing the quasistatistical character of physical societies. These function according to an average or "mean," of change or alteration, reducing the majority of factors of transformation to simple details that can then be ignored. The sole aim, the sole goal of a "society," is to maintain its historic route, the movement of its inheritance, the taking up, the transmission of the acts of feeling that comprise it. In the case of societies such as crystals or rocks, this possibility of persisting requires the power of the average that allows for relevant details to be excluded. At certain moments, when changes of environment become as great as their modes of experience, these changes can impose themselves, no longer leaving any room for the average ignorance that had been maintained up to that point; not being able to transform themselves, these societies are unable to maintain the route that defined their identity.

The stability of living societies, however, is not due to indifference but, rather, to the relevance of their *partiality*. They are essentially, even vitally, *interested* in their environment. It is here that the details of the changes that might appear insignificant for "physical societies" gain their full importance. For living societies, to be interested means "orienting themselves," "choosing," "searching";[72] essentially it is a matter of an activity in relation to a specific environment. Living societies are not simply passively affected by what happens in their environment; they actively reach out to be affected. This is why they form the most fragile of realities within the orders of nature. The environment is not an indifferent succession, overwhelmed by some kind of average, but a collection of questions which will lead the living society to transformations that are internal (changes in its form) or external (changes in elements in the environment). If a society is defined as the endurance of a social order, it is possible to state that living societies are capable of modifying this social order. This capacity is the very condition of their continued existence. Their past is not something that imposes itself but is a virtuality that they will actualize differently on each occasion, depending on the changes in the environment. Living societies allow themselves to be transformed by that which lurks in their interstices and which, in turn, they take up in their historic route.

The question that is to be asked of "living societies" is that of their *consistency*. The consistency of a being can be defined as having "the capacity to conserve its identities across the vicissitudes which result from its relation with other beings."[73] Thus, "each body is provided with a certain degree of consistency."[74] Living societies maintain an order from which they emerge by continually reinvented means, by perpetuating a tradition that defines them. They share a common aim with physical societies, namely, that of persisting, but living societies differentiate themselves from physical ones through the means by which they achieve this. For them, everything happens at the interstitial level, in the empty places in which life lurks,[75] in the intervals between blocks of becoming, and in the zones that separate the several series that are engaged in one persistence. If an individual is a living person, in the same way as a cell is, this is because between the acts that constitute them, and are taken up within them, certain transformations insert themselves, thereby changing their mode of being. These living persons and cells reinvent, in part, the manner in which they inherit themselves.

Physical societies, rocks, or crystals, "are not agencies requiring the destruction of elaborate societies derived from the environment; a living society is such an agency. The societies which it destroys are its food. This food is destroyed by dissolving it into somewhat simpler social elements. It has been robbed of something."[76] Its conditions of existence involve theft and the destruction of elements of its environment. That which is stolen could well be another inferior organism, but "whether or no it be for the general good, life is robbery."[77] What differentiates a crystal from what is living is the interested activity that defines the living. The crystal is indifferent to what it produces and to the effects of the environment in the short term; a "cyclone does not seek out the most heavily populated zone to feed on the ravages it causes. It goes where it goes."[78] But the living require "means for locating, grasping, seducing, capturing, trapping, and pursuing";[79] the history of a living being is the history of "ever more effective modes of destruction"[80] that enable the living being to endure. All the metaphors that can be used to compare the physical and the living risk forgetting what differentiates them: indifference and detachment on one hand, interest and attachment on the other.

Following Stengers, I will refer to this collection of interested and dependent relations between a living being and the environment as "dynamics of infection."[81] They are dynamic because the relations are variable, never established once and for all: what was once an actor later becomes or is, from another perspective, an effect of process. There is no other point of stability than these dynamics themselves, the changing, negotiated relations between the living being and the environment. This leads to a minimal definition of a living being: it is that which *infects* and lets itself be *infected*. I am using the term "infection" in its etymological sense: *in-facere*, to make within, to act in the interior, and more generally, to impregnate, or be impregnated, without, of course, the solely negative connotation of being pathological. Here, the term "infection" is taken in a speculative sense, that is to say, as neutral regarding its consequences for this or that particular living being. Infection can designate both the destruction *and* the transformations of which living beings are capable. It is a matter of designating all those relations of dependence, of activity, of contamination, and the processes of integration—acts of feeling—through which the living being appropriates the elements of its environment—"life is robbery"—and, in turn, transforms them.

Everything happens in encounters. The capacity of a society is relative to its environment and vice versa. It is not possible to get beyond a form of empiricism where that which counts are the interactions in which living beings are engaged. "The point to be emphasized is the insistent particularity of things experienced and of the act of experiencing. Bradley's doctrine—Wolf-eating-Lamb as a universal qualifying the absolute—is a travesty of the evidence. *That* wolf ate *that* lamb at *that* spot at *that* time: the wolf knew it; the lamb knew it; and the carrion birds knew it.[82]

A different wolf, a different environment, a different encounter would entail a different event and different powers. The wolf's power is relative to the power of the lamb and to the place in which their meeting has occurred. None of these terms has any a priori primacy in explaining what has happened. Such dynamics involve a genuine ecology of relations. The analysis so far has remained at only one level—the meeting of one organism with another—but it needs to be generalized to all levels. Each organism, in so far as it is a society, is itself an ecosystem. This generalization of the relations of infection is very close to an idea that can be found in the work of the French biologist Pierre Sonigo. In *Neither God nor Gene*, Sonigo writes, "Cells form a society which resembles that which we find at other levels, in ecology or economics."[83] These are not metaphors but another manner, another way, which is nevertheless also technical, of accounting for the modes of existence of living societies. Hence, "the relations between cells rely on exchanges of resources which are comparable to those which structure ecosystems (food chains) or human societies (economic cycles)."[84] And an entire ecosystem can be found "in each one of us, composed of billions of microscopically small animals, which we call our cells. They live for themselves and not for us. They do not know that we exist."[85]

In opposition to Bradley, Whitehead states that the relation between the wolf and the lamb can be taken up at the level of the billions of cellular societies that constitute an organism. In so far as they are living societies, they take, capture, and destroy other living societies and try, like all the others, to prolong their existence, to endure. Even cells are interested in their environment. That which we think with regard to more complex organisms, we must also think of living beings at the infinitely small scale. They are affected and they affect. Any consciousness that a living being can have of these dynamics is an outcome of such dynamics, and certainly not their origin.

CHAPTER THREE

The Intensification of Experience

~~~~~

So far, I have set a mannerist definition of being against the modern experience of nature that arises from the gesture of bifurcation. There is nothing beyond manners. Mannerism has been offered as a possible and coherent route for thinking a pluralist universe, one that is constituted by a myriad of centers of experience each of which is equally important, equally active, of which the human anthropological experience represents one form but is never able to claim to be either their foundation or model.[1] In order to provide consistency, it has been necessary to relocate all those qualities that have been extracted from things into the interior of existence itself: perspectives, aesthetic sensations, the sense of importance and of value. What is needed is a philosophy that, in its very form, its ambition and its manners of relating to things, can grant due importance to the deeply plural experience of nature. I will call this philosophy "speculative" and will define it through its function: *the intensification of an experience to its maximal point*. In order to outline this function, I will draw on two elements that come from Whitehead's last great work, *Modes of Thought*. When readers and specialists of Whitehead have encountered this book they have either shown little interest—a position that they believe to be justified, as they feel that it involves little more than an attempt to simplify what had already been dealt with more fully in *Process and Reality*—or they are wary of the book, as it is too metaphorical, too lyrical, and seems to introduce more confusion than clarification. However, a new question runs through this book, one that is absent from Whitehead's previous writings and that I will place at the heart of the speculative enterprise: What is it that produces a sense of importance? This question involves a multiplicity of others that provide it with its consistency: Does this sense of importance refer to a particular faculty, a faculty of feeling, imagining, or reasoning that projects its own interests and values onto the things of the world? Or should importance be situated at the heart of existence itself, as if things were important by themselves, independently of the intentions of those who affirm such importance? Does importance vary from one era to another, undergoing historical fluctuations that make us reject as outdated what another era believed to be crucial? In a nutshell, does this sense of importance refer to a human faculty or to a dimension that goes beyond an exclusively anthropological realm?

Before offering a definition, I will start with two contrasts that readily come to mind regarding importance. First of all, importance differs from matters of fact. Whitehead places both at the heart of all experience: "There are two contrasted ideas which seem inevitably to underlie all width of experience, one of them is the notion of importance, the sense of importance, the presupposition of importance. The other is the notion of matter-of-fact."[2] Importance concerns the value of a thing; facts designate brute existence. Such a notion of brute existence is a pure abstraction that comes from an act of simplification carried out by the intellect.[3]

What would a factual existence, one that is essentially, absolutely, without importance, be like? Even if we found an example of such a fact, would we not make the very possibility of such a fact a matter of importance? Would it not confirm or deny the importance of the hypothesis that is being tested? But we could say the same of the concept of importance. What would importance in itself *be*, independently of any situation, of any factual existence? Would it not immediately lose all value if it did not refer, in one way or another, to those beings that support it or make it important? The contrast between importance and matters of fact is not an opposition; it is the highlighting of distinct qualities of experience. Consequently, "there is no escape from sheer matter-of-fact. It is the basis of importance; and importance is important because of the inescapable character of matter-of-fact."⁴ As a result, the notion of importance can be distinguished from another notion with which it is regularly confused: interest. When we say that something is interesting or of interest, are we not, ultimately, saying that it is important? In this sense, does it not have the same value as when we say it matters, that it has importance? Likewise, does the importance that we attribute to a thing not simply refer to the interest that we have in it? However, there is a clear and fundamental difference between these two notions: importance expresses the manner in which an event crystallizes what is at stake beyond its immediate existence hic et nunc. We say of a discovery or an invention that they are important when we wish to highlight the fact they have genuinely changed a situation in the world in which they occur. Whitehead is willing to take up this commonplace view and affirm that the importance of a historical event, for example, is proportionate to the transformations that it produces in the course of history, beyond its own reality. Ultimately, if we extend this view, then we are led to assert that importance is the expression of a "unity of the Universe."⁵ From the moment that a historical event has taken place, all the preceding events seem to converge, retrospectively; the historical event makes them adjust to a new era that has importance precisely because it is essentially a question of the course of the world in which the event is situated but surpassed. The notion of interest is not so broad; it relates to the particularity of an event, to its individuality. If we link what is conveyed by these two contrasts (importance and matters of fact/importance and interest), we arrive at the idea that importance is this unity of the universe, always situated in an actual event.

Whitehead provides a more technical definition: importance "is that aspect of feeling whereby a perspective is imposed upon the universe of things felt."⁶ This definition is somewhat obscure, and Whitehead simply announces it, without looking to justify or develop it, as if the definition were self-evident and no other explanation were necessary. It is true that the terms used, notably those of feelings and perspectives, have been the subjects of numerous analyses in other works. Whitehead dedicates a complete chapter to perspectives in *Modes of Thought*.

Nevertheless, the speed with which this definition of importance is formulated is certainly not justified by the fact that its components have been dealt with elsewhere. I will take this definition as it is given in this passage, without overloading it with other such interpretations. We find that the term "feeling" appears twice, giving the impression of a circular definition that starts with "feeling," with an aspect of "feeling," and ends up with what is "felt" as a perspective upon the word felt. However, the insistence on placing feeling at the heart of the definition has a direct and radical effect. Feeling takes the place of that which, when it comes to importance, is usually ascribed either to consciousness or to intentionality. We can, therefore, infer that the importance of an event is not related to the consciousness that we may have of it, to the intentions that we project on to it, or to the effects that we may foresee or imagine that we can deduce. Whitehead reiterates this point several times, leaving no doubt as to the reason why he gives such a place to feelings: "We put aside, and we direct attention, and we perform necessary functions without bestowing the emphasis of conscious attention,"[7] or again, "A feeling does not in itself involve consciousness."[8] This does not mean that consciousness has no role in relation to importance, but it is neither its origin nor its basis. A sense of the importance of events, a manner of experiencing and feeling what matters (what is important), is prior to any consciousness. This sense of importance indicates a wider dimension than that expressed by consciousness; it can be found in the activity of living: "The sense of importance [. . .] is embedded in the very being of animal experience."[9]

Propositional Lures

However, this placing of importance within feelings, at a level prior to consciousness, leaves a critical question unanswered: How to intensify this sense of importance? If importance is uniquely "that aspect of feeling whereby a perspective is imposed upon the universe of things felt," then where do its increase and its gradation come from? How can events that were previously insignificant grow in importance or, similarly, lose importance after either a longer or shorter period of time? If, as Whitehead's suggests, there is a cosmological element to this defini-

tion, in that it concerns all feelings, then how can we explain the variations, intensifications, reductions, or even ranking of importance? This
question of changes in importance is central to the task of defining the
function of speculative thought. For, if importance is given once and
for all, instantly, for each event, then speculative thought will have no
purpose, except to state that there is importance, but now importance
has become so widespread that it has lost all relevance. I am suggesting
that the unique function of speculative philosophy is to make experience *matter*, to make it important, to intensify it to its maximum. It
is, therefore, the increase in the importance of an experience that is of
interest. Unfortunately, the definition of importance that Whitehead
has given, in so far as it seeks to give a central role to feelings, does not
help us at this point. It needs to be completed.

In *Process and Reality*, Whitehead dedicates an entire chapter to
"propositions." The question of propositions, what characterizes them,
what they require, and their effects, is one of the constants of the work
of Whitehead from the time of *Principia Mathematica* at least. My
aim is neither to trace the history of the concept of "proposition" in
Whitehead's work, nor to establish any links between it and other
philosophical positions that were in evidence when Whitehead was
writing. Nor will I compare Whitehead's "propositions" to other philosophical approaches, such as logic, epistemology, or semiotics, which
also try to grant propositions a fundamental status. My aim is more
precise: to understand how there can be an intensification of experience. For, when he deals with "propositions" in *Process and Reality*,
Whitehead does so in terms of an intensification, as I will demonstrate
shortly. A proposition is not a description of matters of fact, nor is it a
representation, or a judgment; it is a *lure for feeling*.[10] The making of a
proposition is, essentially, the luring of a multiplicity of feelings.

We should consider the term "lure" for a moment, as Whitehead
uses it in a quite particular sense, removing all negative connotations.
In Whitehead's vocabulary, "lure" certainly does not carry the idea of
either an artifice designed to fool someone, or an illusion that masks
reality. For Whitehead, the term is resolutely neutral: a lure incites a
change that can be either positive or negative, according to the circumstances; it entices someone, produces a diversion, modifies the course

of an event, and makes it go in a new direction. Thus, when Whitehead says of propositions that they are "lures for feeling," there is no criticism, no denunciation, intended by his use of this phrase. It simply is a matter of seeing propositions as involving a *capture* or a *grasping*.

In this sense, it is imperative not to confuse propositions with judgments. Their functions complement each other but they are not identical. Thus, Whitehead is particularly virulent in his numerous attacks on those theories that try to make propositions particular instances of judgments. For example, he writes, "Unfortunately theories, under their name of 'propositions,' have been handed over to logicians, who have countenanced the doctrine that their one function is to be judged as to their truth or falsehood."[11] This attack on logic is only a pretext. The problem is much broader and relies upon an illegitimate belief according to which the primary function of a proposition is to be the vehicle for a judgment. This is not to deny completely this aspect of propositions but to limit its relevance: "The doctrine here laid down is that [. . .] 'judgment' is a very rare component, and so is 'consciousness.'"[12] In order to make this difference as telling as possible, Whitehead starkly summarizes, almost to the point of caricature, any conflation of propositions with judgments as being not only illegitimate but almost comical. "The existence of imaginative literature should have warned logicians that their narrow doctrine is absurd. It is difficult to believe that all logicians as they read Hamlet's speech, 'To be, or not to be: . . .' commence by judging whether the initial proposition be true or false, and keep up the task of judgment throughout the whole thirty-five lines. Surely, at some point in the reading, judgment is eclipsed by aesthetic delight."[13] Although the soliloquy is purely theoretical, as a series of statements, it has a function that clearly goes beyond its exclusively verbal expression: the capture of a multiplicity of feelings. When judgment is taken as operating in an overly narrow dimension, it loses the imaginative leap implied in the proposition. The feelings that are implied in the soliloquy might well be of different orders: aesthetic, moral, axiological, and, in certain cases, even logical. But they run through the thirty-five verses. These verses cannot be judged individually nor through a series of judgments that would somehow reveal the true meaning of these feelings. Taken as a proposition, the soliloquy produces a clear and dramatic intensification of the feelings that they lure. These feelings aim at "value as elements in feeling."[14] In this sense, it would be absurd to ask if the propositions uttered during Hamlet's soliloquy are true or false, as they have a completely different function: increasing the importance of the experience that is embodied in the feelings, and to which these feelings are attached.

Alternative Worlds

The function of propositions is to produce an intensification of feelings. But a question still remains: How do they manage to do this? What, exactly, do propositions put into perspective that enables them to induce such an intensification of these feelings? To be precise, what is captured in these propositions when they act as lures, so that these feelings now acquire a dimension that was previously unknown to them? Let us take a new example: the Battle of Waterloo.

> This battle resulted in the defeat of Napoleon, and in a constitution of our actual world grounded upon that defeat. But the abstract notions, expressing the possibilities of another course of history which would have followed upon his victory, are relevant to the facts which actually happened. We may not think it of practical importance that imaginative historians should dwell upon such hypothetical alternatives. But we confess their relevance in thinking about them at all, even to the extent of dismissing them.[15]

Using the example of a battle to explicate a theory of propositions is not without certain dangers, for it accentuates the idea of an irruption, of an event as a rupture that leads to a new epoch; this might seem to situate the concept of propositions in a predominantly anthropological framework. This example of a battle is both pertinent and risky. However, the way in which Whitehead presents this example, the elements that he musters, the terms that he uses, allow us to pinpoint the speculative dimensions of propositions that are required for the argument that I am making.

Propositions link actual feelings (subjects) and possible worlds (predicates). When he mentions the Battle of Waterloo, Whitehead introduces something very specific that forms one of the ongoing concerns of his theory of propositions and which is the central point of the question of intensification, according to the role that I want to give it in the framework of speculative propositions. He raises the idea that another "course of history was possible." This is neither a slogan nor a simple assertion that could be added to any interpretation of historical events—that things could have been otherwise. This insistence on another course resonates at the heart of an event. The question of another course of action, for either the event or for history, is an urgent one that is posed in each act that makes up the battle, at all levels of its existence, in both the daunting possibility of defeat and the hesitations of the soldiers at the very moment that they occur. Running through these hesitations, a multiplicity of possible worlds is attached to each act as it plays out: the French armies come out victorious; they are defeated; the coalition crumbles and a new equilibrium comes to light; the battle continues and carries on and victory no longer makes any sense.

Without doubt, Whitehead knew of Renouvier only through the praise that William James had given him.[16] Nevertheless, the emphasis that Whitehead gives to envisaging other courses of history, taking account of events as they could have been, is not so different from a genre established by Renouvier in his book *Uchronie*.[17] What is the function of these "uchronies"?[18] Are they not just abstract exercises, whose aim is to relativize events and remind us that history is not totally determined in the moment that it is made? Uchronies are much more substantial than this; they are not simply pedagogical or heuristic tools. They are the condition of what I have called the rise in importance, of intensification. This point is key to the function of speculative thought, so there is a need to be more precise. If the outcome of the battle had always been written, if it merely followed a routine course that had been established once and for all, if it actualized only historical over-determinations, then all the value of the event would dissipate, and with it our heritage. This would make the battle only one event in a linear sequence; it would miss precisely what makes *this* occasion *that* historical moment where the creation of our actual world was played out. These possibilities dramatize, and thereby intensify, the defeat.

However, it is important not to exaggerate the status of these possible worlds. They would be only pure, general, abstractions if their existence were not always local, situated in concrete events: the hesitation in *this* action, the worry felt at *that* moment, the bifurcations that come to be in *this* lack of action. Thus, of all the deeds, of all the actors, of all the actions, it is necessary to state that they are "a hybrid between pure potentialities and actualities."[19] In this sense, speculative propositions require a milieu that gives them their consistency. They do not make decisions for the world; they articulate events differently. In order for the idea of another course of history to acquire any consistency, it must lure, or capture, the real worries, the effective feelings, that partially preexist them. These feelings are the feelings of the battle that develop in the memories of the participants, in literary works, in books written by historians as they depict its unfolding. This group of physical, aesthetic, and imaginative feelings form the milieu of new propositions that persevere with regard to the battle. When the "imaginative historian," as described in Whitehead's example, meditates on these other courses of history, life is given to the possibilities that are attached to that historical occasion. The propositions that the historian develops, and to which the historian is closely tied, will gain in importance as they bring together the hesitations that accompanied this singular historical event. The importance of propositions is, therefore, related to the relevance of the articulations that they produce.

It is certainly legitimate to ask who judges this relevance. Where might we find the criteria that would allow us to say that one proposition is more relevant than another, and according to what perspective would we be able to evaluate the extent of the articulations that they entail? If, in reality, a plurality of possible worlds is formed in the course of the battle, if these possible worlds come to be confirmed or refuted by the histories that tell us of this battle, how can we establish any differences between them? Should we take them all as equal, as having the same level of existence, the same force and intensity? In the passage that I have cited, Whitehead gives us a way of responding: "This battle resulted in the defeat of Napoleon, and in a constitution of our actual world grounded upon that defeat."[20] It is not in the battle itself that its importance can be found. This would be a rather uninspiring finding. Intensification carries all the hesitations that run through the battle, all the possibilities that animate it and that come to destabilize its grandeur.

Ultimately, the relevance of a proposition is related to the constitution of our actual world. We cannot go beyond this. This "other course of history," these alternative worlds that are dramatized by the "imaginative historian" who develops such uchronies—these have no other function than making sense of our actual world, what it inherits, the fragility of the history from which our world is derived, the possibilities that continue to have a latent presence. These past conditionals, these "could have beens," are focused on the constitution of our actual world, a world-in-the-making, with its hesitations, its latent bifurcations, its tendencies, which says nothing definitive beyond itself.

It is now possible to return to my initial definition of the function of speculative philosophy: the intensification of an experience to its maximal point. Importance is given. It belongs to all existence in so far as importance embodies a particular perspective on the universe that is expressed in each of the elements of the cosmological dimensions it inherits. The ways of feeling, of connecting, of grasping, and the importance that these assume, are constitutive of nature itself. It is not that there are primary qualities on one side and secondary qualities on the other; rather, there are the specific articulations of each existent that are the affirmations of what matters here and now. But even if importance is everywhere, it is nevertheless up to us to intensify it, to give to importance all the dimensions that it requires. In a word, to establish its *value*. Even if this question has been posed in terms of a historical event, it is clearly not limited to the realm of history and its legacies, as it concerns our contemporary experience and the possibilities that animate it. This is an inherently moral activity whose maxim could be "Whether we destroy, or whether we preserve, our action is moral if we have thereby safe-guarded the importance of experience so far as it depends on that concrete instance in the world's history."[21]

Notes

INTRODUCTION

1   For more on this subject, see Emilie Hache, *Ce à quoi nous tenons: Proposi-tions pour une écologie pragmatique* (Paris: Les Empêcheurs de penser en rond, 2011).

2   Beyond the purely philosophical sphere, I am thinking of works such as Con-rad Hal Waddington, *The Strategy of Genes: A Discussion of Some Aspects of Theoretical Biology* (London: George Allen & Unwin, 1957); Joseph Need-ham, *The Refreshing River* (Nottingham, UK: Spokesman, 1943); and also Ilya Prigogine and Isabelle Stengers, *La Nouvelle alliance: Métamorphose de la science* (Paris: Gallimard, 1986).

3   For more on this, see Isabelle Stengers, *Thinking with Whitehead* (Cam-bridge, MA: Harvard University Press, 2011).

4   This is a notion that I have taken from Deleuze's description, in *The Fold*, of Leibniz's approach as a philosophy of manners. "The Stoics and Leibniz invent a mannerism that is opposed to the essentialism first of Aristotle and then of Descartes. Mannerism as a composite of the Baroque is inherited from a Stoic mannerism that is now extended to the cosmos. A third great logic of the event will come with Whitehead"; Gilles Deleuze, *The Fold* (Lon-don: Athlone Press, 1993), 53. Deleuze also cites an extract from Leibniz's *New Essays on Human Understanding* in which Leibniz writes, "The kinds and degrees of perfection vary up to infinity, but as regards the foundation of things. The foundations are everywhere the same; this is a fundamental maxim for me, which governs my whole philosophy. But if this philosophy is the simplest in resources it is also the richest in kinds [of effects]" (*Fold*, 150). In this sense, I have no hesitation in situating this project in a mannerist philosophy in the forms of the neo-monadology that can be found as much in Whitehead as in Tarde or Ruyer.

CHAPTER 1 | THE COSMOLOGY OF THE MODERNS

1   Alfred North Whitehead, *The Concept of Nature* (Cambridge: Cambridge University Press, [1920] 1964), 7.

2   Alfred North Whitehead, *Science and the Modern World* (New York: Pelican Mentor, [1925] 1948), 17–18.

3   Whitehead, *Science and the Modern World*, 19.

4   Alfred North Whitehead, *Modes of Thought* (Cambridge: Cambridge University Press, 1938), 34.

5   Whitehead, *Science and the Modern World*, 8.

6   Whitehead, *Concept of Nature*, 30.

7   Maurice Merleau-Ponty, *Nature: Course Notes from the Collège de France* (Evanston, IL: Northwestern University Press, 2003).

8   See, for example, Jean Wahl, *Vers le concret: Etudes d'histoire de la philosophie contemporaine, William James, Whitehead, Gabriel Marcel* (Paris: J. Vrin, 2010); and Jean Wahl, *Les philosophies pluralistes d'Angleterre et d'Amérique* (Paris: Empêcheurs de penser en rond, 2005).

9   Félix Cesselin, *La philosophie organique de Whitehead* (Paris: Presses Universitaires de France, 1950), 21.

10 Whitehead, *Science and the Modern World*, 19. Other brief references can be found, notably in *Modes of Thought*, principally in the chapter "Nature Lifeless."

11 I have taken this term from the work of Gilles Châtelet, particularly his *Figuring Space: Philosophy, Mathematics, and Physics* (Dordrecht: Kluwer, 2000).

12 John Locke, *An Essay concerning Human Understanding* (London: Penguin Books, 1997 [1690]), 135, book 2, chapter 8.

13 Locke, *Essay concerning Human Understanding*, 135.

14 Whitehead, *Science and the Modern World*, 56.

15 Whitehead, *Science and the Modern World*, 18.

16 Raymond Ruyer, "Ce qui est vivant et ce qui est mort dans le matérialisme," trans. M. Halewood, *Revue philosophique* 116, nos. 7–8 (1933): 28.

17 Ruyer, "Ce qui est vivant," 28.

18 The question of organicism is widely discussed in *Science and the Modern World*. For an analysis of the influence of Whitehead's organicist approach on the field of contemporary biology, see Donna Haraway, *Crystals, Fabrics, and Fields* (Berkeley, CA: North Atlantic Books, 2004).

19   Isabelle Stengers, "Diderot's Egg," *Radical Philosophy* 144 (2007): 7–15.

20   Locke, *Essay concerning Human Understanding*, book 2, chap. 8, §10.

21   Whitehead, *Concept of Nature*, 42.

22   Whitehead, *Concept of Nature*, 29–30.

23   Whitehead, *Concept of Nature*, 31.

24   Isabelle Stengers, *The Invention of Modern Science*, trans. Daniel W. Smith (Minneapolis: University of Minnesota Press, 2000), 84 (italics in original).

25   Stengers, *Invention of Modern Science*, 85 (italics in original).

26   Quentin Meillassoux, *After Finitude* (London: Continuum, 2008), 1.

27   Meillassoux, *After Finitude*, 1.

28   Meillassoux, *After Finitude*, 1.

29   Whitehead, *Science and the Modern World*, 58.

30   Ruyer, "Ce qui est vivant," 28–49.

31   Whitehead, *Science and the Modern World*, 50.

32   Whitehead, *Science and the Modern World*, 51.

33   Alfred North Whitehead, *Adventures of Ideas* (Cambridge: Cambridge University Press, 1933), 200–201.

34   Wahl, *Vers le concret* (2010), 133.

35   Whitehead, *Adventures of Ideas*, 132–33.

36   Whitehead, *Concept of Nature*, 20.

37   Ruyer, "Ce qui est vivant," 28–49.

38   Whitehead, *Science and the Modern World*, 58–59.

39   Translator's note: location meant as localization.

40   Whitehead, *Concept of Nature*, 54.

41   Alfred North Whitehead, *Process and Reality: An Essay in Cosmology*, ed. David Ray Griffin and Donald Sherburne, Gifford Lectures of 1927–28. Corrected ed. (New York: Free Press, [1929] 1978), 7.

42   Henri Bergson, *Creative Evolution*, trans. Arthur Mitchell (London: Palgrave Macmillan, 2007), 214. The translation has been slightly altered; the original reads, "It is undeniable that if there be no entirely isolated system."

43   Bergson, *Creative Evolution*, 329.

44   Bergson, *Creative Evolution*, 329.

45   Bergson, *Creative Evolution*, 329.

46 Bergson, *Creative Evolution*, 328.

47 Bergson, *Creative Evolution*, 336.

48 Whitehead, *Process and Reality*, 209.

49 Henri Bergson, *The Creative Mind: An Introduction to Metaphysics* (Mineola, NY: Dover, 2007), 159 (italics in original).

50 Bergson, *Creative Mind*, 160 (italics in original).

51 Bergson, *Creative Mind*, 36.

52 Wahl, *Vers le concret* (2010), 123–24.

53 Whitehead, *Modes of Thought*, 67.

54 Whitehead, *Science and the Modern World*, 34.

55 Whitehead, *Science and the Modern World*, 84.

56 Whitehead, *Science and the Modern World*, 59.

57 Whitehead, *Science and the Modern World*, 56.

58 Whitehead, *Science and the Modern World*, 56 ("arises" in the original).

59 Whitehead, *Concept of Nature*, 163.

60 Whitehead, *Process and Reality*, 49–50.

61 Whitehead, *Concept of Nature*, 20–21.

62 Whitehead, *Science and the Modern World*, 57.

63 Whitehead, *Science and the Modern World*, 57.

64 See Bertrand Saint-Sernin, *Whitehead, un univers en essai* (Paris: J. Vrin, 2000), for an account of the relations between phenomenology and the philosophy of Whitehead.

65 Whitehead, *Concept of Nature*, 3.

66 Whitehead, *Concept of Nature*, 148.

67 Whitehead, *Modes of Thought*, 2.

68 William James, *Essays in Radical Empiricism* (London: Longmans, 1912), 42.

69 Gilles Deleuze, *Difference and Repetition* (London: Athlone Press, 1994), 284–85.

70 Whitehead, *Concept of Nature*, 14–15.

71 Whitehead, *Concept of Nature*, 15.

72 Whitehead, *Concept of Nature*, 54.

73 Wahl, *Vers le concret* (2010), 136 (translator's translation).

74   Gilles Deleuze, *The Fold* (London: Athlone Press, 1993), 76.

75   For more on the theory of events in *The Concept of Nature* and how this is taken up in later works such as *Process and Reality*, see Wahl, *Vers le concret* (2010).

76   Whitehead, *Concept of Nature*, 165.

77   Whitehead, *Concept of Nature*, 166.

78   Whitehead, *Concept of Nature*, 166.

79   Whitehead, *Concept of Nature*, 166.

80   Whitehead, *Concept of Nature*, 166.

81   Whitehead, *Concept of Nature*, 167.

82   An inheritance of Whitehead's idea that persistence involves a trajectory of reprises can be found in Bruno Latour's *An Inquiry into Modes of Existence: An Anthropology of the Moderns* (Cambridge, MA: Harvard University Press, 2013).

83   Whitehead, *Concept of Nature*, 165.

84   Whitehead, *Concept of Nature*, 167.

85   I have taken the expression "plane of nature" from Deleuze and Guattari. For example, in *A Thousand Plateaus*, they write, "We call this plane, which knows only longitudes and latitudes, speeds and haecceities, the plane of consistency or composition (as opposed to the plan[e] of organization or development). It is necessarily a plane of immanence and univocality. We therefore call it the plane of Nature, although nature has nothing to do with it, since on this plane there is no distinction between the natural and the artificial. However many dimensions it may have, it never has a supplementary dimension to that which transpires upon it. That alone makes it natural and immanent." Gilles Deleuze and Félix Guattari, *A Thousand Plateaus* (London: Athlone Press, 1988), 266.

86   Whitehead, *Concept of Nature*, 169.

87   Gottfried Wilhelm Leibniz, *New Essays on Human Understanding* (Cambridge: Cambridge University Press, 1981), 74.

88   Whitehead, *Concept of Nature*, 151.

89   Whitehead, *Concept of Nature*, 29.

90   Whitehead, *Concept of Nature*, 48.

91   Whitehead, *Concept of Nature*, vii–viii.

1   Alfred North Whitehead, *Process and Reality: An Essay in Cosmology*, ed. David Ray Griffin and Donald Sherburne, Gifford Lectures of 1927–28, corrected ed. (New York: Free Press, [1929] 1978), 167.

2   William James, *Collected Essays and Reviews* (New York, Longmans, Green, 1920), 443–44.

3   For a discussion of the relation between aesthetics and ontology in Whitehead with regard to the question of feelings, see Steven Shaviro, *Without Criteria: Kant, Whitehead, Deleuze, and Aesthetics* (Cambridge, MA: MIT, 2009).

4   Whitehead, *Process and Reality*, 41.

5   René Descartes, *Meditations on First Philosophy* (Cambridge: Cambridge University Press, 1911), 10–11.

6   Whitehead, *Process and Reality*, 41.

7   Whitehead, *Process and Reality*, 176.

8   Alfred North Whitehead, *Symbolism: Its Meaning and Effect* (New York: Macmillan, 1927), 42.

9   George Santayana, *Scepticism and Animal Faith: Introduction to a System of Philosophy* (Mineola, NY: Dover, 2003).

10   Whitehead, *Symbolism*, 42.

11   Whitehead, *Symbolism*, 34.

12   Whitehead, *Symbolism*, 44.

13   Gilles Deleuze, *The Fold* (London: Athlone Press, 1993), 78.

14   I have, elsewhere, provided a more detailed account of the question of possession in the work of Tarde. See Didier Debaise, "The Dynamics of Possession: An Introduction to the Sociology of Gabriel Tarde," in *Mind That Abides: Panpsychism in the New Millennium*, ed. David Skribna, 221–30 (Amsterdam: John Benjamins, 2008).

15   Gabriel Tarde, *Monadology and Sociology* (Melbourne, Aus.: re.press, 2012), 54.

16   Tarde, *Monadology*, 52.

17   Tarde, *Monadology*, 54.

18   Whitehead, *Process and Reality*, 21.

19   Whitehead, *Process and Reality*, 21–22.

20 Whitehead, *Process and Reality*, 87.

21 Gottfried Wilhelm Leibniz, *Discourse on Metaphysics* (La Salle, IL: Open Court, 1902), 15.

22 Leibniz, *Discourse on Metaphysics*, 14.

23 Leibniz, *Discourse on Metaphysics*, 14.

24 Deleuze, *Fold*, 81.

25 Whitehead, *Process and Reality*, 226–27.

26 Whitehead, *Process and Reality*, 40.

27 Whitehead, *Process and Reality*, 24.

28 Whitehead, *Process and Reality*, 43.

29 This is given as *subiecutum* in the original.

30 Martin Heidegger, *The End of Philosophy* (Chicago: University of Chicago Press, 2003), 27.

31 Whitehead, *Process and Reality*, 151.

32 For a discussion of chains and transitions of experience, see William James, *Essays in Radical Empiricism* (London: Longmans, 1912), particularly essay 2, "A World of Pure Experience." And, for a contemporary reading of chains of experience, see Bruno Latour, "A Textbook Case Revisited: Knowledge as Mode of Existence," in *The Handbook of Science and Technology Studies*, ed. Edward Hackett et al., 83–112, 3rd ed. (Cambridge, MA: MIT Press, 2013).

33 Alfred North Whitehead, *Modes of Thought*, 32.

34 Whitehead, *Modes of Thought*, 33.

35 For an account of the question of individual perspective within the history of modern biology, see Scott Gilbert, "A Symbiotic View of Life—We Have Never Been Individuals," *Quartely Review of Biology* 87, no. 4 (2012): 325–41. Gilbert writes, notably, that "for animals, as well as plants, there have never been individuals. This new paradigm for biology asks new questions and seeks new relationships among the different living entities on Earth. We are all lichens" (336).

36 Raymond Ruyer, "Ce qui est vivant et ce qui est mort dans le matérialisme," *Revue philosophique* 116, nos. 7–8 (1933): 28–49.

37 Ruyer, "Ce qui est vivant," 40 (translator's translation).

38 Whitehead, *Modes of Thought*, 33.

39 Whitehead, *Modes of Thought*, 33.

40 I have taken the term "consolidation" from Eugène Dupréel: "Théorie de la consolidation: Esquisse d'une théorie de la vie d'inspiration sociologique," *Revue de l'Institut de Sociologie* 3 (1934): 1–58.

41 Whitehead, *Modes of Thought*, 208.

42 This is very close to what Étienne Souriau calls "solicitudinary." For more on this, see Étienne Souriau, *Avoir une âme: Essai sur les existences virtuelles* (Paris: Les Belles Lettres, 1938); and Étienne Souriau, *The Different Modes of Existences* (Minneapolis, MN: Univocal Publishing, [1943] 2015), which has a magnificent introduction written by Bruno Latour and Isabelle Stengers.

43 Whitehead, *Process and Reality*, 222.

44 Deleuze, *Fold*, 78; the punctuation has been altered slightly.

45 Whitehead, *Process and Reality*, 39.

46 Whitehead, *Process and Reality*, 39.

47 Whitehead, *Process and Reality*, 39.

48 Whitehead, *Process and Reality*, 93.

49 Plato, *Timaeus and Critias* (Oxford: Oxford University Press, 2008), 44–45.

50 Plato, *Timaeus and Critias*, 44–45.

51 Whitehead, *Process and Reality*, 44.

52 Whitehead, *Process and Reality*, 25.

53 Translator's note: I have chosen to retain the English word "instauration" here. This is not a commonly used term in English, but it is a word with a long history. Indeed, Francis Bacon (1561–1626) used the term in the title of his incomplete major project, *Instauratio Magna*, translated as *The Great Instauration*. The term is intended to invoke both an establishment and a renewal. The *Oxford English Dictionary* defines it as follows: "The action of restoring or renewing something." This term is also used in a very technical way by Souriau in *The Different Modes of Existence* (2015); see also the introduction to this book by Bruno Latour and Isabelle Stengers.

54 Alfred North Whitehead, *The Concept of Nature* (Cambridge: Cambridge University Press, [1920] 1964), 169.

55 Alfred North Whitehead, *Science and the Modern World* (New York: Pelican Mentor, [1925] 1948), 88.

56 For a more detailed analysis of the classification of eternal objects in Whitehead, see William Christian, *An Interpretation of Whitehead's Metaphysics* (New Haven, CT: Yale University Press, 1959).

57 Deleuze, *Fold*, 80.

58   Deleuze, *Fold*, 79.

59   Alfred North Whitehead, *Adventures of Ideas* (Cambridge: Cambridge University Press, 1933), 354.

60   Whitehead, *Process and Reality*, 10.

61   Whitehead, *Process and Reality*, 23.

62   Whitehead, *Process and Reality*, 44 (italics in original).

63   Jean Wahl, *Vers le concret: Études d'histoire de la philosophie contemporaine* (Paris: J. Vrin, 1932), 135 (translator's translation).

64   Samuel Butler, *Life and Habit* (London: Trübner, 1878), 124.

65   Whitehead, *Process and Reality*, 89–90.

66   Whitehead, *Process and Reality*, 90.

67   Conrad Hal Waddington, *The Strategy of Genes: A Discussion of Some Aspects of Theoretical Biology* (London: George Allen & Unwin, 1957). Regarding the inheritance of Whitehead's philosophy in biology, the work of Joseph Needham should also be noted; see *The Refreshing River* (Nottingham, UK: Spokesman, 1943); and *Order and Life* (Cambridge: Cambridge University Press, 1936), and an account of this influence can be found in Donna Haraway, *Crystals, Fabrics, and Fields* (Berkeley, CA: North Atlantic Books, 2004).

68   Whitehead, *Process and Reality*, 43.

69   Translator's note: Up to this point in this passage, I have used the word "milieu" to translate the original French *milieu*. I have now switched to "environment" to translate the same word, as in the following quotation Whitehead talks of the "social environment" and "environment," rather than "milieu." It is worth bearing the connotations of both terms in mind.

70   Whitehead, *Process and Reality*, 100.

71   Whitehead, *Process and Reality*, 102.

72   I will not go into much detail on the transformations of knowledge that are linked to the "interested" character of living beings. For a fuller discussion, see Vinciane Despret, *Quand le loup habitera avec l'agneau* (Paris: Les empêcheurs de penser en rond / Le Seuil, 2002). Despret places the concept of a "proposition of existence" at the center of a genuine "culture" of living. She writes, "The propositions of existence of which our 'histories' are the vectors, the manners of enlisting animals in these histories and the practices which arrange them, are not addressed to a docile and mute world, a simple support for our representations. Our histories which concern them are not indifferent to them" (26; translator's translation). It is a matter of highlighting the interested character of living beings to the questions that are asked of them.

73 Eugène Dupréel, "La consistance et la probabilité constructive," *Lettres* 55, no. 2 (1961): 1–38 (translator's translation).

74 Dupréel, "La consistance," 1–38 (translator's translation).

75 For a more detailed analysis of the relations involved in interstitial life, see my discussion in "A Philosophy of Interstices: Thinking Subjects and Societies from Whitehead's Philosophy," *Subjectivity* 6, no. 1 (2013): 101–11.

76 Whitehead, *Process and Reality*, 105.

77 Whitehead, *Process and* Reality, 105.

78 Isabelle Stengers, *Thinking with Whitehead: A Free and Wild Creation of Concepts* (Cambridge, MA: Harvard University Press, 2011), 313.

79 Stengers, *Thinking with Whitehead*, 313.

80 Stengers, *Thinking with Whitehead*, 313.

81 Stengers, *Thinking with Whitehead*, 157–63.

82 Whitehead, *Process and Reality*, 43.

83 Jean-Jacques Kupiec and Pierre Sonigo, *Ni Dieu ni gène: Pour une autre théorie de l'hérédité* (Paris: Points/Seuil, 2000), 129 (translator's translation).

84 Kupiec and Sonigo, *Ni Dieu ni gène*, 129 (translator's translation).

85 Kupiec and Sonigo, *Ni Dieu ni gène*, 129 (translator's translation).

CHAPTER 3 | THE INTENSIFICATION OF EXPERIENCE

1 For more on this subject, see the works of Eduardo Viveiros de Castro, principally *Cannibal Metaphysics* (Minneapolis: Minnesota University Press, 2014), and "Exchanging Perspectives," *Common Knowledge* 10, no. 3 (2004): 463–84.

2 Alfred North Whitehead, *Modes of Thought* (Cambridge: Cambridge University Press, 1938), 5.

3 Through an analysis of Whitehead's texts, Bruno Latour has outlined the relations between the bifurcation of nature and the question of matters of fact and "matters of concern." See Latour, "What Is a Style of Matters of Concern? Two Lectures in Empirical Philosophy," *Spinoza Lectures* at the University of Amsterdam in 2005, published as an independent pamphlet, Van Corcum, Amsterdam, 2008.

4 Whitehead, *Modes of Thought*, 5.

5 Whitehead, *Modes of Thought*, 11.

6 Whitehead, *Modes of Thought*, 15.

7 Whitehead, *Modes of Thought*, 15.

8   Alfred North Whitehead, *Process and Reality: An Essay in Cosmology*, ed. David Ray Griffin and Donald Sherburne, Gifford Lectures of 1927–28, corrected ed. (New York: Free Press, [1929] 1978), 256.

9   Whitehead, *Modes of Thought*, 12.

10 Whitehead, *Process and Reality*, 184. See also Isabelle Stengers, *Thinking with Whitehead: A Free and Wild Creation of Concepts* (Cambridge, MA: Harvard University Press, 2011).

11 Whitehead, *Process and Reality*, 184.

12 Whitehead, *Process and Reality*, 184.

13 Whitehead, *Process and Reality*, 184–85.

14 Whitehead, *Process and Reality*, 185.

15 Whitehead, *Process and Reality*, 185.

16 James mainly praises Renouvier with regard to his position on "phenomenism." See, for example, footnote 18 of his essay "The Place of Affectional Facts in a World of Pure Experience." See also the letters between James and Renouvier, published by Ralph Barton Perry as "Correspondance de Charles Renouvier et de William James" in *Revue de Métaphysique et de Morale* 36, no. 1 (1929): 1–35. And, more generally, see Jean Wahl, *The Pluralist Philosophies of England and America* (Charleston, South Carolina: Nabu Press, [1925] 2011).

17 Charles Renouvier, *Uchronie: Esquisse historique apocryphe du développement de la civilisation européenne tel qu'il n'a pas été, tel qu'il aurait pu être* (Paris: Fayard, 1988).

18 Although the term "uchronie" is related to "utopia," it also has a significant difference. "Uchronie" involves the rewriting of history based on a change in a past event.

19 Whitehead, *Process and Reality*, 185–86.

20 Whitehead, *Process and Reality*, 185.

21 Whitehead, *Modes of Thought*, 20.

Bibliography

Bergson, Henri. *Creative Evolution*. Translated by Arthur Mitchell. London: Palgrave Macmillan, 2007.
———. *The Creative Mind: An Introduction to Metaphysics*. Mineola, NY: Dover, 2007.
Butler, Samuel. *Life and Habit*. London: Trübner, 1878.
Castro, Eduardo Viveiros de. *Cannibal Metaphysics*. Minneapolis: University of Minnesota Press, 2014.
———. "Exchanging Perspectives." *Common Knowledge* 10, no. 3 (2004): 463–84.
Cesselin, Félix. *La philosophie organique de Whitehead*. Paris: Presses Universitaires de France, 1950.
Châtelet, Gilles. *Figuring Space: Philosophy, Mathematics, and Physics*. Dordrecht: Kluwer, 2000.
Christian, William. *An Interpretation of Whitehead's Metaphysics*. New Haven, CT: Yale University Press, 1959.
Debaise, Didier. "The Dynamics of Possession: An Introduction to the Sociology of Gabriel Tarde." In *Mind That Abides: Panpsychism in the New Millennium*. Edited by David Skribna, 221–30. Amsterdam: John Benjamins, 2008.
———. "A Philosophy of Interstices: Thinking Subjects and Societies from Whitehead's Philosophy." *Subjectivity* 6, no. 1 (2013): 101–11.
Deleuze, Gilles. *Difference and Repetition*. London: Athlone Press, 1994.
———. *The Fold*. London: Athlone Press, 1993.
Deleuze, Gilles, and Félix Guattari. *A Thousand Plateaus*. London: Athlone Press, 1988.
Descartes, René. *Meditations on First Philosophy*. Cambridge: Cambridge University Press, 1911.
Despret, Vinciane. *Quand le loup habitera avec l'agneau*. Paris: Les Empêcheurs de penser en rond / Le Seuil, 2002.
Dupréel, Eugène. "La consistance et la probabilité constructive." *Lettres* 55, no. 2 (1961): 1–38.

———. "Théorie de la consolidation: Esquisse d'une théorie de la vie d'inspiration sociologique." *Revue de l'Institut de Sociologie* 3 (34): 1–58.

Hache, Emilie. *Ce à quoi nous tenons: Propositions pour une écologie pragmatique.* Paris: Les Empêcheurs de penser en rond, 2011.

Haraway, Donna. *Crystals, Fabrics, and Fields.* Berkeley, CA: North Atlantic Books, 2004.

Heidegger, Martin. *The End of Philosophy.* Chicago: University of Chicago Press, 2003.

James, William. *Collected Essays and Reviews.* New York: Longmans, Green, 1920.

———. *Essays in Radical Empiricism.* London: Longmans, 1912.

Kupiec, Jean-Jacques, and Pierre Sonigo. *Ni Dieu ni gène: Pour une autre théorie de l'hérédité.* Paris: Points/Seuil, 2000.

Latour, Bruno. *An Inquiry into Modes of Existence: An Anthropology of the Moderns.* Cambridge, MA: Harvard University Press, 2007.

———. "A Textbook Case Revisited: Knowledge as Mode of Existence." In *The Handbook of Science and Technology Studies,* edited by Edward Hackett et al., 83–112. 3rd ed. Cambridge, MA: MIT Press, 2013.

———. *What Is a Style of Matters of Concern? Two Lectures in Empirical Philosophy.* Amsterdam: Van Gorcum, 2008.

Leibniz, Gottfried Wilhelm. *Discourse on Metaphysics.* La Salle, IL: Open Court Publishing, 1902.

———. *New Essays on Human Understanding.* Cambridge: Cambridge University Press, 1981.

Locke, John. *An Essay concerning Human Understanding.* London: Penguin Books, [1690] 1997.

Meillassoux, Quentin. *After Finitude.* London: Continuum, 2008.

Merleau-Ponty, Maurice. *Nature: Course Notes from the Collège de France.* Evanston, IL: Northwestern University Press, 2003.

Needham, Joseph. *Order and Life.* Cambridge: Cambridge University Press, 1936.

———. *The Refreshing River.* Nottingham, UK: Spokesman, 1943.

Perry, Ralph. "Correspondance de Charles Renouvier et de William James." *Revue de Métaphysique et de Morale* 36, no. 1 (1929): 1–35.

Plato. *Timaeus and Critias.* Oxford: Oxford University Press, 2008.

Prigogine, Ilya, and Isabelle Stengers. *La Nouvelle alliance: Métamorphose de la science.* Paris: Gallimard, 1986.

Renouvier, Charles. *Uchronie: Esquisse historique apocryphe du développement de la civilisation européenne tel qu'il n'a pas été, tel qu'il aurait pu être.* Paris: Fayard, 1988.

Ruyer, Raymond. "Ce qui est vivant et ce qui est mort dans le matérialisme." *Revue philosophique* 116, nos. 7–8 (1933): 28–49.

Saint-Sernin, Bertrand. *Whitehead, un univers en essai.* Paris: J. Vrin, 2000.

Santayana, George. *Scepticism and Animal Faith: Introduction to a System of Philosophy*. Mineola, NY: Dover, 2003.

Scott, Gilbert. "A Symbiotic View of Life—We Have Never Been Individuals." *Quartely Review of Biology* 87, no. 4 (2012): 325–41.

Shaviro, Steven. *Without Criteria: Kant, Whitehead, Deleuze, and Aesthetics*. Cambridge, MA: MIT, 2009.

Souriau, Étienne. *Avoir une âme: Essai sur les existences virtuelles*. Paris: Les Belles Lettres, 1938.

———. *The Different Modes of Existence*. Minneapolis, MN: Univocal, [1943] 2015.

Stengers, Isabelle. "Diderot's Egg." *Radical Philosophy* 144 (2007): 7–15.

———. *The Invention of Modern Science*, translated by Daniel W. Smith. Minneapolis, MN: University of Minnesota Press, 2000.

———. *Thinking with Whitehead: A Free and Wild Creation of Concepts*. Cambridge, MA: Harvard University Press, 2011.

Tarde, Gabriel. *Monadology and Sociology*. Melbourne, Aus.: re.press, 2012.

Waddington, Charles. *The Strategy of Genes: A Discussion of Some Aspects of Theoretical Biology*. London: George Allen & Unwin, 1957.

Wahl, Jean. *Les philosophies pluralistes d'Angleterre et d'Amérique*. Paris: Empêcheurs de penser en rond [1932] 2005.

———. *Vers le concret: Études d'histoire de la philosophie contemporaine*. Paris: J. Vrin, [1932] 2010.

Whitehead, Alfred North. *Adventures of Ideas*. Cambridge: Cambridge University Press, 1933.

———. *The Concept of Nature*. Cambridge: Cambridge University Press, [1920] 1964.

———. *Modes of Thought*. Cambridge: Cambridge University Press, 1938.

———. *Process and Reality: An Essay in Cosmology*. Edited by David Ray Griffin and Donald Sherburne. Gifford Lectures of 1927–28. New York: Free Press, [1929] 1978.

———. *Science and the Modern World*. New York: Pelican Mentor, [1925] 1948.

———. *Symbolism: Its Meaning and Effect*. New York: Macmillan, 1927.

Index